I CANNOT HEAR YOU
BUT I CAN HEAR GOD

I CANNOT HEAR YOU
BUT I CAN HEAR GOD

PHILLIP HASSALL
and Sylvia Mandeville

HODDER AND STOUGHTON
LONDON SYDNEY AUCKLAND TORONTO

British Library Cataloguing in Publication Data

Hassall, Phillip and Mandeville, Sylvia
  I cannot hear you but I can hear God.—
  (Hodder Christian paperbacks)
  1. Christian life
  I. Title   II. Mandeville, Sylvia
  248.4   BV4501.2

ISBN 0-340-38268-6

Contents

All Bible references unless otherwise stated are taken from the New International Version.

To save embarrassment I have changed almost everybody's name in this book.

Many thanks are due to the following for helping me over the years with the Bible, and especially Adrian Pope – he was the first to help. Also to: Phillip and Sharon Carter, Alan and David Champneys, Martin Chapman, Barry and Maureen Chaseley, Andrew and Deborah Clarke, Katherine Day, Martin Dobson, Tim Ellwood, Pastor Peter Goodchild, Susan Haizelden, Graham and Malcolm Hills, Mark Howgill, John, David and Patricia King, Carole Liston, Andrea and Deane McSkimming, Ray Moxham, Christine Olney, Michael Padmore, Kay Sharp, Jenny Shilling, Susan Steel, Peter Wagstaff, Deborah Whitehead, Elizabeth and John Winter, and many others.

Phillip Hassall

Preface

My first memories of Phillip are simply of the deaf boy over the road. I guess that back in 1972 I was too young to understand the problems of being deaf and hence avoided Phillip whenever I could, which was most of the time. I first got to know Phillip through the scouts. He struck me as a boisterous person who often got into trouble. He was very strong. Using this strength was often the only outlet for his frustrations.

I remember particularly one summer scout camp, when he was in my patrol. He resented authority and refused to do what he was told by a patrol leader. Much of the time, due to his strength, he would get away with it. One evening things came to a head and when the scout leader tried to reprimand him, he turned violent.

However those days are gone. Today Phillip is a shining example of the transforming power of Jesus Christ in the lives of those who believe in Him.

This book tells the story of the frustrated deaf boy who found peace and hope with the all absorbing love of the Lord Jesus Christ.

David Champneys
January 1984

Foreword

'When Phillip was only a few days old I held him in my hands and said, "Lord, he's yours. I give him to you, and to show I mean it, I'm coming back to you too."'

Phillip's mother

'We may never know the reason now. Perhaps we'll find out the reason later.'

Phillip's father

1. A Day to Remember

It was my favourite day. The day the mobile library came to our village. I was almost five and I loved going down with my mother to choose books. We went every week, climbing up the steps into the large silvery van, squeezing our way to the end where the children's books lay waiting.

But on that day in October I didn't want to go. I had a headache. A bad headache and I kept complaining about it as we looked at the books. The sun was shining as we walked home but I didn't notice. All I could think about was the pain in my head. In the afternoon my grandparents were coming to see me. Normally I looked forward to their visits, but not on that day. Instead of sitting on Grandpa's knee and being galloped vigorously to market I sat quietly on my own not bothering to play or talk.

'There's something the matter with you!' Mum said and she put me to bed. She was not too worried. Both my Dad and my brother Greg were ill with mumps. I must be sickening for it too. By the evening I was feeling worse. My temperature shot up. Mum phoned the doctor but he didn't think it worth coming out to see me. An attack of mumps may be painful but it is not dangerous.

The pain in my head got more than I could bear.

'Mummy! Mummy! Mummy!' I cried. I wanted her near me. Those are the last words I can clearly remember hearing. All through the night I cried and screamed with the pain. By now I was too ill to be aware of the comings and goings in the house, the worried conversations between my parents, the panic in their eyes. Finally the next day the doctor came. Diagnosis was not simple. There was mumps in the house. Three days earlier I had had my whooping cough injection. Perhaps I was reacting to that. I often had asthma. Was this a bad attack? We had not long come back from holiday. Had I picked up a virus from the rather murky swimming pool?

The next thing I was aware of was strange men wrapping me in a blanket and gently lifting me on to a stretcher and carrying me into an ambulance. My mother sat by me on the journey. I looked up through the window. All I could see were trees moving and the sky above. Mum and the ambulance man smiled at me as we rushed along through the country lanes.

When we arrived at the hospital I was rapidly transferred from the stretcher to a high iron bed, on my own in a small room. Something had happened to me. My limbs lay limp by my side. I could hardly move at all. Doctors and nurses came to look at me. I could not understand what was happening. Everyone had to wear a gown and mask, even Mum. I lay there crying and unhappy.

After some painful tests the doctors told my mother that I was dangerously ill with meningitis. Unless they could get my temperature down I would die or perhaps suffer from brain damage. On the other hand to treat the meningitis they would have to give me massive doses of streptomycin which also carried its own risks with side effects which might possibly disturb my hearing.

I was at death's door. Mum phoned our vicar and other friends at St Andrew's, the church where we all went. She asked them to pray for me to live. Later Dad told me that he and Mum were too choked to pray proper prayers, though on the night I almost died they managed to pray somehow. All our friends prayed for me as I was too young to die.

And so the treatment began. The first injection of streptomycin was given. My temperature slowly began to fall. I was going to live. I lay there still very ill, crying. The nurses and I did not seem to get on very well with each other. They said they had told me about ringing the bell when I wanted to go to the toilet. I had no memory of being told. They thought I was just being awkward. What upset me too was that they would not let me get out of bed for the toilet. I had to use a bed pan which I hated.

I'm not sure when it happened but one day I realised that my hearing had gone. Mum was talking to me or was she playing a game? Her mouth was talking but no sounds were coming out. She went on talking and I tried to make out what she was saying but I could not hear a thing. Because I was so ill it was not immediately obvious to anyone that I was deaf. It was thought that I was too weak to respond to people or that I was just plain difficult. Mum knew better. She began to suspect that something was wrong. She spoke to the Sister but she was convinced that I was a spoilt child and just playing up. The next time the consultant came round Mum spoke to him.

'I'm sure Phillip is deaf,' she said.

The doctors stood round my bed and one of them put his hand on my head and around my ears. I could not hear what they were saying. I thought they were talking to themselves.

'We'll soon see if he's deaf,' one of the doctors said and he reached up to switch on the hospital radio. Naturally my eyes followed the movement of his hand.

'No, he isn't deaf,' the doctor said, 'see how he heard the radio.'

My mother was not impressed. She was sure I was deaf. She could tell that I was puzzled by what was going on and that I did not understand her when she spoke to me.

My world had suddenly gone completely strange. Not a sound was coming out of people's mouths, yet they kept moving them. I could not understand what they were trying to say. I spoke very little. I was unnerved. I felt that even my speech could not be understood. Something cheered me up in my isolated ward. A wonderful present of a Chitty Chitty Bang Bang car with all the people in it. I was delighted and played every day with it. All these years later, I've still got three of the people left, but not the driver.

Apart from the shock of being deaf, another thing worried me. Why didn't Dad and my brother Greg come to visit me? Because they had mumps they were not allowed to see me. Perhaps Mum had explained it but perhaps at the time I had been too ill to take in the information. Now it was too late. I could not hear any explanations. I could only lie there and worry.

Something else upset me. Would my parents ever want me home again? I had been a long time in hospital. Perhaps they did not want me any more. When I was better would I be homeless? Where would I go and who would look after me?

Mum was having as distressing a time as I was. Not only was she desperately worried about me but she was also torn in her loyalties. Dad and Greg needed some care and attention at home, some meals cooked for them and some shopping done.

Neighbours and friends from church were wonderful, popping in with home-baked pies and taking away loads of washing, but they could not do everything. Mum could not drive the car and Dad was not well enough to take her. Every day Mum had to make the journey at eight in the morning and back again at about eight thirty in the evening by bus. She was so upset and worried that she used to pray that she would not meet anyone she knew on the bus. She could not face talking about what was happening. The weather was beautiful at this time and every evening there was a huge burning harvest sun in the sky. If ever she did meet anyone she would say, 'The sun is making me all red,' to cover up the fact that she had been crying.

As I gradually got better I began to feel lonely in my little room. One day I sat up in bed and peered around me. Through the glass I could see other children in the next ward. I saw that they were all together and that I was all on my own. When a nurse came in I got down quickly. I wished I could go and play with them.

Whenever my mother or grandparents came to see me I could sense a profound sadness about them. They were all worried about my deafness. But life in hospital had to go on, and the regular injections of streptomycin were part of the routine. My leg was a funny shape from having so many. One day a nurse came in very cheerfully and announced that I need not have any more injections. From now on I could have it all from a spoon. Mum was sure she was wrong as she thought streptomycin could only be given by injection. Aware of her concern, when I saw the spoon instead of the needle I refused to take it. The nurse insisted. I made such a fuss that Mum had to hold me down. I kept my mouth tightly closed. The nurse resorted to the old trick of holding my nose. I was soon gasping for breath and had to open my mouth. In popped spoonful number one. Two more arrived in the same way. Quite unsuspecting, the nurse turned to get spoonful number four and stood there poised in her spotless white uniform. Then I let her have it. I spat out all over her the three spoonfuls of medicine which I had been saving up. She was smothered in bright pink spots. Angrily she rushed away to change. A few moments later Sister appeared. In silence my medicine was given by injection, nor was any attempt ever made to do otherwise.

The days passed and I was still frail. It seemed as if I was in there for ever. Sometimes just as Mum arrived the doctors came to examine me and Mum had to go out. How I hated that. I wanted her to be there. Mum was still trying to get some sense out of them about my being deaf. Even they were beginning to think she might be right, but they would not commit themselves. The nursing staff certainly had no doubts. They knew I was just a horror and making the most of all the attention. Deaf I was not.

At last I was well enough to go home. I was just a thin shadow of the bonny child I'd been a few weeks before. In those brief days my whole world had changed. Nothing would ever be the same again. What was waiting for me in my silent future?

2. Strange New World

Fish fingers. That was all I could think about when I got home. I must have fish fingers for my tea. After weeks of hospital food I was determined to have something I fancied. Of course poor Mum hadn't got a thing in the house. Any reserves had long since been eaten and no one had had time to go shopping. Anxious that my welcome home should be successful, Mum rang up a friend who quickly came to the rescue. Soon a large packet of my favourite fish fingers was sizzling in the frying pan.

Dad marked the occasion by taking a family photograph. We all knew that from now on our family life would be different.

The first thing I had to do was to learn to walk again. Not only was I weak from having been so ill and from being in bed for so long, but whatever had affected my hearing had also affected my sense of balance. Whenever I tried to walk I wobbled and fell over. Although I was almost five I had to suffer the indignity of being pushed around once more in an old pushchair. But it did get me out into the fresh air and down to the mobile library again.

My young brother Greg was a great help to me. He didn't worry about my being deaf. He had no hang-ups. He found his own way of communicating with me. Soon with his help I was running around just like him, though even now I sometimes ruck up carpets with my feet through a poor sense of perspective. If only my parents could have known, as they so anxiously watched my first cautious steps, that one day I would be competing in the two hundred metres race at the Crystal Palace.

Apart from the delight at being home again and being able to tumble about with Greg I found my new silent world strange. I would suddenly catch Mum, Dad and Greg laughing uproariously at something. What were they laughing at? I hadn't heard any joke. If I asked them they would have to struggle with signs to explain to me. But an impromptu joke soon loses its humour when retold in this way. Of course they had to carry on chatting to themselves some of the time, but I began to feel the icy pains of isolation.

The first few weeks were a period of adjustment for all of us. If any one wanted to speak to me they had to touch me to get my attention. This can be annoying. Most children develop a habit of ignoring many of the remarks made to them by parents while they are involved in an interesting game. They conveniently go deaf when they are told to go to bed or to clear the table or to tidy up. But when you are totally deaf you cannot escape like that. It is not so easy to ignore a firm poke in the ribs!

I gradually got used to them touching me whenever they wanted to speak to me and I began without realising to do the same to them. I acted as though they were deaf and touched them before I spoke. Mum, who was exhausted after the weeks of stress found this particularly infuriating. Fortunately as I grew older I dropped the habit.

Although we all found it hard to communicate with each other, in many ways I was fortunate. I had had four years, almost five years of hearing.

To a deaf person every hearing year is a golden year. I had already picked up a wide vocabulary normal for my age. I was able to express myself simply and I had heard all the sounds necessary for speech. A child who is born deaf has a much greater handicap. Some sounds are very difficult to make if they have never been heard. Others, for example, *sh*; *oo*; *ph*; are difficult to lip read. Even now when someone is speaking if I do not know the context I may mistake the word *choose* for *Jews* or *news*. It takes a long time to learn to lip read as well as to speak clearly. I find the thing to do is to catch several words out of a sentence and try to make sense of it. Some people are easier to understand than others. They seem naturally to form words with their lips more clearly.

Looking back now I can see that my parents must have gone through a lot of suffering which they hid from me. Dad says that many people prayed for me and he was grateful to them. He said, 'Mum and I used to cry in bed every night, but I didn't ever cry properly. Several years later I nearly had a breakdown. I don't think I was a Christian at the time. It's hard to tell, but praying was difficult. In situations like that you don't need words to pray. Your heart cries. God hears those sort of prayers.'

My mother suffered too. She says that if she had not been a Christian she could never have coped with everything. 'Whenever Dad and I prayed we felt we could not understand the reason why it had happened. But I didn't want to blame God or the doctor or anyone. We prayed that we would be able to accept it. I didn't go to pieces. There was too much to do. I just had to get on.'

Mum tried to explain to me how it was that I'd caught meningitis. She said that the germs had come from someone else and had rapidly spread in my body, making me ill. I did not understand what she was trying to say. It wasn't until years later that I was able to grasp how germs spread. I felt very angry then to think what had happened to me, but now I forget all about it.

One of the things which upset Mum most was that she had not taught me to read before I went deaf. She could so easily have done. I was a bright and eager four and three quarter year old, I was used to handling books and reading pictures, I was a confident chatter box. I was a model of reading readiness. But Mum had been firmly told by the teacher at the local school where I was due to start the following January that no way was she to teach me to read before I crossed the school threshold. The local school used the Initial Teaching Alphabet, a phonetic system of teaching reading with specially printed books. The teacher felt that amateur attempts by mothers to get the child to read would end in confusion. If only Mum had ignored them. I would have had a flying start. As it was, although I was almost five, I could not read a word. This meant that if all other methods of trying to explain something to me failed, I could not even read a few words written down for me to make things clear.

Mum was also worried that the meningitis might have damaged me mentally. She had heard various horrific stories, and as soon as I was well enough she did her own private tests on me to check that I was all right. She gave me a hard Donald Duck jigsaw to do which I'd always loved doing before I was ill. She held her breath to see whether I could still do it. Fortunately my brain had not been damaged and I slotted all the bits together rapidly.

What astonished my parents at this time was how high and dry they were left by the medical profession in caring for me. The whole family had gone through the traumatic experience of my illness. Not only I but all of them had to come to terms with my deafness which the hospital only cautiously acknowledged a fortnight later when I returned for a final check. Because I was physically better from meningitis I was catapulted out of hospital. The only advice given to my parents by our family doctor was to keep me amused. My mother did that and more as a normal part of bringing me up anyway. What they needed was sensible advice, professional help and encouragement. In the circumstances my parents did the best they could. They got hold of books on how to help deaf children. They read as widely as they could. They did as much teaching of me as they could fit into the day.

They taught me by signs and gestures how to lip read phrases such as, 'Go to sleep now', 'Time to get up', and 'Eat your dinner'. Dad also worked out a system with me. He would get my attention and say one important word like 'Football'. When I'd understood that, he would say the next word, 'Spurs'. I would grin and then he would say, 'Match'. When he saw that I'd grasped that word he would say, 'Saturday'. Conversations were slow but we gradually made progress.

Mum found that she could not bring herself to put any records on the record player. She found it too upsetting to think that she could hear the music and I could not. But I liked her to put records on. I was fascinated by the automatic movements of the record and the arm of the player. Also I could sometimes sense the vibrations from the music and an occasional low sound.

One day we went to visit a friend whose son was also deaf. We had a good time playing together. Somehow we managed to lock ourselves in his bedroom. When we found we could not unlock the door we panicked and shouted and yelled. Both mothers knew it was no good giving us instructions through the door. In the end the boy's mother had to climb in through the window. We were still shouting, not knowing whether anyone had heard us. It is at times like these that deaf people feel so helpless and cut off.

Perhaps now would be a good time to tell you a little more about myself and my family. I was born in a small hospital in Kent in 1964 on December 24th so I was very nearly a Christmas baby. Mum told me how on Christmas Day when she was in hospital she realised that although she had rushed round at home and left everything organised for Christmas, she had completely forgotten to get a present for my Dad. When he came visiting, Mum said to him, 'Phillip is your present.'

A few days later Mum was looking at me in the hospital. She was so overcome with the wonder of having a baby that she held me in her hands and prayed, 'Lord, he is yours. I give him to you, and to show I mean it, I'm coming back to you too.' And Mum meant that prayer. She went to the little hospital service for thanksgiving for a new baby. When she got home she began going regularly to the early morning communion service at the local church. Dad used to have a lie in, while Mum took me off wrapped up in a huge old-fashioned pram, which was always a problem to get through the church doors. It's a rather special feeling to think that as a new baby I was used to bring my mother back to the Lord.

When I was three I began Sunday school. I'm glad I did because it meant that I had heard a little bit about Jesus before I went deaf. When I got back from church I often used to play vicars, using my long-suffering brother Greg as the congregation. By now my father had begun to go to church too, so Christian influences came early into my life.

We were a normal happy family and when I was four we all went off for a wonderful holiday at Christchurch. It was our last holiday before I went deaf. I had a glorious time swimming almost all day long, playing on the swings and seesaws. It was good to have those happy sunny memories and photographs to help us through that difficult autumn.

Once I was able to walk again and was strong, I went back to my play group. I felt unhappy there. I could not hear anything and children came and tried to speak to me but I could not understand them. They found it difficult too. We all felt unhappy. But the time was coming when I had to start school. I had to face the big wide world.

3. My First School

Everything had been planned for me to go to the village school. I had visited it with my mother, met my teacher and looked round the classroom. I already knew some of the children there. Others whom I knew at the play group would be starting with me in January. Now everything had to be changed. The first day of term had come and gone. I was in urgent need of specialist help. My speech was already beginning to deteriorate. Because I could not hear conversation around me all day long I was forgetting words I'd once known. Cadences were fast disappearing from my speech. As the weeks went by certain small words began to be lost. Instead of saying, 'I want a drink', I would say, 'I want drink'. For 'I go to bed', I would say, 'I go bed'. Gradually instead of 'I want drink', I slipped into 'Me want drink'. The ends of certain words got lost and to correct this my mother would rhyme words which I was still saying properly with words I was mis-saying. I was certainly in need of school, but not the local school. With no special equipment they could not cope with a child who so recently had gone profoundly deaf.

At last the professionals began to take an interest in me. My future had to be sorted out. In an amusing essay, my mother wrote an account of our experiences:

It is time for Phillip to go to school, and so the Education Authority looms large, and presents itself as an elderly, retired gentleman. In one brief visit he tries to teach us something about lip reading. Most of what he had to offer was common sense which we knew already through our experience. What the gentleman advised was to hold objects close to the lips and then pronounce the word. Phillip was able to tell him the name of the objects as he already knew the names of the farm animals which were being shown to him. He also mentioned about getting the attention of the child by touching and by making sure that his eyes were on you. Also the fact that by facing the light, features show more clearly than if you have your back to it. At this time Phillip's vocabulary was a good average for a five year old. He knew colours, could count and could read and write his name. I mention this because most teachers of the deaf handle children who are born deaf and the vocabulary rate is very much lower, some are as low as twenty-five words at five years.

Next I was referred to the ear nose and throat unit of another local hospital to have my hearing tested and to have an ear piece moulded for a hearing aid. It was here for the first time that my parents received help and guidance. The staff were very co-operative. Mr Edwards dealt with audiograms, the graphs which indicate the degree of hearing loss. I was a shy child and found the tests difficult to understand. I was not sure what was expected of me on these occasions. I think because Mr Edwards was slightly deaf himself he was particularly kind and sympathetic. He had to tell us that I had a ninety-nine per cent hearing loss. No one has a hundred per cent hearing loss. You would go mad if you were in total silence. As I have said before I can respond to vibrations and some extremely low sounds.

It was at this unit that we were told how the ear works, and what had happened to my ear. We were also given details and advice about using a hearing aid. Some people think that hearing aids are an almost magical cure for deafness. They are not. What they do is to amplify sounds, all sounds, not just the speech which you do want to hear, but background noises also which you do not want to hear.

A committee made up of teachers, the education officer and a doctor decided that because of the traumatic way in which I had gone deaf I should not go immediately to a residential school for the deaf, but to the Slade County Primary School some distance away which had a partially hearing unit for children aged two and half years to eleven years. Because I had such a good knowledge of speech and language I was classed as partially hearing.

My parents took me over to Slade one day to look around. It was playtime when we arrived and all the children were running about. We walked through their playground games and found the PHU. I liked what I saw. It was a fairly new unit with a small amount of good equipment. There was some sound proofing to deaden echo and sound rebound. Everything looked like an ordinary classroom, which was the whole idea, so that we felt as much as possible like the hearing children in the rest of the school.

Once we had had a good look round we talked to one of the teachers. My father asked about hearing aids. The teacher showed him the NHS Mednesco hearing aid which I would be using. I looked at it and did not think much of it. I asked my father what it was for. He said, 'That is for you.' I turned away and thought to myself, 'I hate it!'

The teacher went on to explain that the loop system was available in one classroom. This is the method in which pupils wear earphones over their hearing aid ear piece, and are connected to the teacher's microphone. When she speaks to them, outside sounds like the scraping of a chair on the ground or a plane going overhead are eliminated. Only the teacher's voice can be heard.

I could not understand everything the teacher was saying, but I was quite happy with my visit.

We went home and talked it all over. The next thing to do was to go and buy my new uniform. That was fun. I was sorry though that I would be going to school so far away and without any of my friends.

Mum and Dad were still trying to come to terms with the fact that my deafness was permanent. For weeks after I got home from hospital they kept doing tests on me to see whether my hearing had come back or improved. One evening when I was in bed, my father went up into the loft unknown to me. Mum was in my bedroom when I suddenly looked up to the ceiling and pointed, saying something about Daddy being in the loft. They were so excited. They thought I had heard something. The next night Dad went up to the loft again. This time Mum realised that I had not heard a sound, but that I had sensed the vibrations of the footsteps overhead. My parents lived on the edge of hope for a long time.

I had enjoyed my first visit to Slade and looked forward to starting school. On the first day my parents took me over in the afternoon. I had missed the beginning of term and was the only pupil joining the school at that time. I was proudly wearing my new uniform, a green jumper and tie, and grey shorts. My parents had a chat with the teacher and then I said goodbye to them in the playground. They kissed me and told me that they would see me at tea time. I would be coming home with other children in a taxi. When they had gone I felt sad being left there. I cried because I missed my parents looking after me and because I was so young.

The teacher soon settled me into my place and my first lesson began. I tried very hard to lip read. I found that I could speak to other children who were not totally deaf. There was no sign language used. We were taught lip reading which is good. At the end of my first day the teacher took me to the car park where the taxi was waiting. Other children from the PHU got in too. When I arrived home I felt quite happy and had my tea. A few weeks later I made friends with several children and they are still my friends even now. Some of them I met years later at further stages of my education.

The teachers soon found that the first hearing aid I had been given was of no use to me. Not a sound could I hear with it. Although I hated wearing it the teachers made sure that I did. It served no purpose from a hearing point of view but it did indicate to others that I was deaf. It was just a visual aid. Back I had to go to the hospital to be tested again and to be fitted with another hearing aid, this time a larger Philips model. I could hear occasional isolated sounds with this.

I had difficulties with one of my teachers there because I did like to do things my way! Whenever I was asked to do a project on a certain subject I would always want to do it on something else. With give and take on both sides we slowly learned to work together. I also learned to read. My mother cannot work out how it was possible for a deaf child to do this and I can't remember how it happened. All I know is that I can read.

As I look back I see that I was fairly happy at Slade. I stayed there until I was eight and a half. I got on well with the other partially hearing children but I found it harder to communicate with the hearing children. It was the old problem: many of them assumed that talking between us was impossible.

Life at home carried on much as usual with all of us slowly adjusting to my deafness. A further extract from my mother's essay gives revealing glimpses of our life at that time:

> During the years the audiograms were still negative, though Phillip was more co-operative. Speech was deteriorating and heads turned when Phillip spoke. Deaf children are never quiet, in fact are over noisy. We were getting used to this.
>
> We were now able to tell people how to communicate with Phillip. Most people have a feeling of fear at first. This is understandable as it is something they are unfamiliar with. Most people are sympathetic but at first look at Phillip as if he is an exhibition model. They will ignore the child and talk through the parents. A smile goes a long way, so does patience.
>
> When left alone people usually manage to communicate. If I am there Phillip will often look at me, almost like a translator. I sometimes look the other way, to force

him to cope and to give him confidence. Greg communicates well but has a sign language all of his own. He finds this most useful when he wants to do something with Phillip without my knowledge. Phillip forgets that we can hear and gives the game away by laughing. Phillip has learnt to use vibrations, movements and expressions.

By the time I was eight the teachers realised that I was only marking time at Slade. I needed more specialist teaching. The unit was geared to the partially hearing and so was no real help to me. Lengthy discussions began as to where I should go. Two boarding schools in a seaside town were suggested.

Meanwhile we had moved from the familiar village where I had lived all my life to a nearby country town. On the day of the move I left for school in the morning in the usual taxi. I was wondering how I would get to school from the new house. As I thought about it I realised that some of the children at Slade came from the same town in another taxi, so perhaps I would be travelling with them. At the end of the day my parents met me with the car. In it was my brother and our pets. Then we drove to our new house. It was about seven miles away. The house looked quite good and I liked it. The next day I set out for school and as I had supposed it was in another taxi. When it arrived I discovered that my best friend Jonathan Bird was already in it.

The move meant changing churches too. I had done well at St Andrew's, the church in the village. The Sunday school teachers had known me since before I had gone deaf and although they could not understand my difficult and muddled speech they did not mind. I had even won a prize for attending a hundred times. It was a large book called *Bible Stories from the Old Testament*.

Here in the town I didn't settle in very well at the new church. We all missed our old friends. I found the new Sunday school boring and when I looked round at the children and the people running it I hated it all, because it was nothing like my old Sunday school and I could not

understand what was happening. The people tried to be
kind but it took them a long time to grasp that I was totally
deaf and what my needs were. They took time to try to talk
to me but I was still not happy there. I could see people
smiling at me, but I wondered what they were smiling
about. Perhaps they were trying to say that Jesus loved me,
but no one ever said it in actual words, to me.

If ever I was out shopping in the town with my parents I
hated meeting people because they would talk and talk, on
and on. They might smile occasionally at me but they would
never ask me any questions or wait for me to give them any
answers. Oh, how boring all that waiting was! Sometimes I
patted my parents to let them know that I wanted to go
now, but they carried on talking. Of course I did not speak
very much, because my speech was not very good. It was
hard work to bother to talk to anyone.

At school I was working harder but still I did not make
much progress. One of the problems was that I could not
get the volume of my own speech loud enough. It was
becoming imperative for me to move. One day we set off
by car to visit the two boarding schools suggested to my
parents. The first one was on the outskirts of the town. We
looked around the classrooms and bedrooms. When we got
to the dormitories I saw how crowded they were. I thought
to myself that I did not like them.

A teacher showed me round and explained all about the
rules for putting socks out for the wash on Mondays,
Wednesdays and Fridays. I realise now that boarding
schools have to have routine for getting clothes washed, but
somehow this rule dismayed me. I thought the school was
not up to much. By the time we had completed our tour of
inspection of the first school we were too late to visit the
second one. My parents asked me what I thought about the
first school and I told them that I didn't like it at all.

About a week later we set off once more to the sea and
the second school. I liked the town very much. When we
came to the school I thought it looked strange. It was not all
in one building but was made up of various houses going up

a steep hill. But it was still a school. Curious. I thought that if any of the classrooms were in a house at the top of the hill children would have to make a lot of effort to get there.

When we arrived my parents left me to look round while they talked to the headmaster. I enjoyed myself. Some of the pupils came and talked to me without sign language. This encouraged me. The teaching must be good if only lip reading was allowed. About half an hour later my parents came to fetch me. They told me that they had seen the bedrooms and other classrooms including the gym and some of the playing fields. So we went off in the car, talking about the school as we went. I agreed that I would like to go there even though it was a boarding school. Little did I know what eventful years lay ahead of me there, both good and bad.

So I spent my last term as a day boy in the PHU at Slade. On the final day I packed up my books, pens and pencils. I said goodbye to everyone and caught the taxi for the last time. I talked all the way to my friend Jonathan. I tried to forget about school but underneath I was feeling very sad.

Before I tell you about life in a boarding school I must tell you about a very special friend.

4. Lady and Me

It was when I was seven that I met one of the most important friends in my life. I did not know how much she was going to mean to me. Not far from our house I frequently saw a beautiful sheep dog. Whenever I could, I patted it. Secretly I longed to own a dog just like that, but I never told my parents. Perhaps they noticed how much fuss I made of the collie. Perhaps someone had told them what a help a dog could be to a deaf person. I don't know the reason, but they told me that sometime, they would get me a dog. I was so excited. What sort would it be? When would we get it?

One day we all went out by car into the country. My parents had seen an advertisement for some puppies. When we arrived at the house where they were for sale the owner took us out to the back. I couldn't believe my eyes. There running round the garden with the mother dog was a litter of black and white collie puppies. They were exactly like the dog I loved so much down the road. The owner held on to the mother while Greg and I ran up and down with the puppies yapping at our feet. I tried to pick one up that I liked but it ran off to hide in its large kennel. Nothing I did would make it come out again. We played with all the others and finally I chose a lovely one which I called Lady.

We took her home and she was great fun. She played in the garden most of the time and was very lively. Sometimes she nipped us, but she was not being naughty because at that time she did not have very sharp teeth. What she did enjoy doing was biting our toys. Whenever she could get hold of it she would nibble my best cowboy hat. Finally I gave up trying to keep it out of her way and gave it to her.

As soon as she was old enough I began to train her. I would call 'Come here', and she came, 'Sit', and she would sit. To help train her I played a ball game. I would get her to sit down next to me. Then I would put my hand about six inches from her eyes. This meant, 'Don't move until I say.' Next I would throw the ball and she learned not to move or run after it. When I saw that she had not moved, I would call out, 'Go,' and off she went to get the ball. It was sometimes difficult to remove the ball from her mouth. I had to keep saying, 'Leave, Lady . . . leave,' to her. I also taught her, 'Get into your basket,' and many other commands. If I were to train another dog now I would do it even better because I can speak more clearly. I would be able to use more tones in my speech.

Through training Lady and romping around with her she became my best friend. I didn't have trouble lip reading her! A wag of the tail or a begging look in her eyes and I could tell what she wanted. I'm sure too that she realised that I was deaf. It was difficult sometimes to teach her when and when not to bark. If all the family was at home and some one knocked on the door, Lady would bark and bark. My mother would tell her to stop, because she went on for so long and so loudly. But when I was alone in the house, it was important that Lady should bark. No way could I hear a ring at the bell or a knock. Once when I was quite small I was alone in the house for a short while and some people rang the doorbell. Lady took no notice. They rang again and this time Lady reacted. She barked and barked very loudly. I could feel the vibrations painfully in my ear. I could also see her getting excited. I rushed to the door and was able to answer the ring once I'd pulled Lady into the kitchen.

On one occasion she was barking furiously and I went to the door. Through the shaded glass I could see a big heavily-built man. This time I did not shut Lady in the kitchen. I held tightly to her collar as I opened the door. If the man was dangerous Lady could attack. It was only the electricity meter reader. I told him I was deaf and that I would bring him the keys to the garage where the meter was. I shut the door and put Lady in the kitchen and went out with the keys. Through having Lady on occasions like this I could answer the door and learn how to cope with callers just like other children have to.

Years later after Lady had died two friends of mine called round. They knew I was going to be alone in the house as my parents were away on holiday. As they walked up the drive they suddenly remembered the problem. No Lady to bark when the doorbell rang. How were they to get me to hear? It was no use phoning to say answer the door. It was no use knocking. To their relief at that moment I just happened to look out of the window and saw them. But the incident highlights the problems the deaf have of enjoying normal social contact. There are special lights you can get which come on when the door bell rings, but we have never had one fitted.

What I loved doing most with Lady was going off on long walks. She loved it too. I was very strict with her and did not let her run in and out of other people's gardens. Nor did I let her eat grass or anything else which might cause her a stomach upset. The rest of the family let her eat grass. They said it was all right, but I didn't agree.

One day out in the country we came to some farm sheds. I went in to explore, leaving Lady to wait. She lay down on an old door which had fallen to the ground. As I came back into that part of the shed I saw it would make a very good photograph. There was Lady in the foreground on the door and beyond her was the sunny outside world. I was very pleased with it when it was printed.

As I write these memories about Lady I find it hard to keep back my tears. I loved her so much and she helped me in many ways which even members of the family could not have done. Especially when I was away at boarding school I enjoyed coming back to her every weekend and playing with her.

When Lady was eleven years she began to feel unwell.

She was not her usual bouncy self. She had a severe stomach upset. I was due one Sunday to leave home for college. Before I went to the station I went out of the back door and Lady came up to me. I knew she was ill. I stroked her slowly and firmly. Then I kept my hand still on her back and prayed for her. I asked for her healing. I was sure that she would get better. I was so sad because of her illness. So I left home for a week at college and did not say farewell to her.

The following weekend I arrived home and sat down for tea. I waited expectantly for Lady to rush in and greet me as usual, but she did not come. Lady, my dog as dear to me as any human, where was she? I began to weep. I was very upset and could not eat my tea. My mother came into the room and I said 'Where's Lady?'

Mum said, 'She's dead. She got very ill. We had to take her to the vet. The only thing he could do for her was to put her to sleep.' I was so upset I was beside myself. My mother tried to comfort me. 'Lady is in heaven,' she said. I had prayed so much. I could not believe that she had died. On that Saturday morning I was due to help my father on the allotment but I was too distressed and in tears. My father let me sit alone quietly and did not make me work with him.

Just recently a new society has been launched to provide dogs for deaf people in the same way that guide dogs are provided for the blind. The idea originated in America. It is called Hearing Dogs for the Deaf.[1] Various firms and food manufacturers and local charities provided the funds to train the first dogs. It is a costly business training a dog and for that reason only the best animals are chosen. Pedigree doesn't matter but a high degree of inquisitiveness to sound and a friendly temperament are important. It has been found that mongrels are bright and suitable for the job.

[1] Hearing Dogs for the Deaf,
  2 Chinnor Hill,
  Chinnor,
  Oxfordshire.

After training, each dog is matched to its new owner with special visits to the home to make sure that not only will it be looked after well, but that the dog's talents are made full use of. Some dogs are trained to respond to a baby crying, others to the doorbell etc., according to what is needed.

When I think of all the fun, help and enjoyment I've had from Lady, I'm glad to think that there is now a Society which will provide similar pleasure to others.

5. Away to Boarding School

For several weeks before the September term began my mother and I were busy buying piles of new school uniform. Boarding school seemed to need far more pairs of socks and pants than I'd been used to. When they'd all been marked with my name, I helped Mum pack. I don't think I realised quite what going away to boarding school meant. Perhaps it would be like going on holiday? I was to be a weekly boarder coming back every Friday on the school coach which ran up to Tunbridge Wells.

At last the day came and we set off one Sunday afternoon in my parents' blue Hillman Imp. Greg my brother came too. He wanted to see where I was going to be staying. When we arrived, we were not sure where to go and stood around wondering what to do. Then someone took charge of us and I was taken up to my bedroom and shown my bed. It was a small school with only about a hundred pupils and the accommodation was divided between three houses. One house had the younger boys and all the girls. The other two houses had the older boys. I found that I was the youngest boy in my house. I was only eight and all the others were eleven and older. The matron chatted to my parents and Mum told her that I was a good sleeper. Like other pupils there I had my favourite teddy bear with me.

After looking round the dormitories we went downstairs and someone told my father that I should need pocket money, so he pulled some money out of his pocket and gave me fifteen pence (quite enough in those days). Then it was time to say goodbye. Before they left, my parents reminded me that they would see me again on Friday afternoon. It sounded a long way off.

As soon as they had gone one of the older pupils took care of me and showed me all over the school. This took a long time and kept my thoughts busy and away from thinking about my parents. I saw the games room which had three different-sized snooker tables. The smallest was for us younger children. The others were larger but about four times smaller than the professional snooker tables. I immediately wanted to have a game even though I didn't know any of the rules. The boy who was taking me round told me what they were and I understood a little, enough to play for a while.

When supper time came, tears filled my eyes, because I was too young to be alone and away from parents for the first time. That night I cried and cried. I could not stop and the night seemed very long. In the morning I felt better and began the day more cheerfully. To begin with we had assembly with songs and prayers, followed by lessons. I settled down to work hard. I discovered that some of the children used sign language, which at first I did not understand, though after a few months I became familiar with it. I was worried about being at this school. I was not sure that it would be good for me. I feared that I might get into trouble in the future.

At last my first week was over. It was Friday. In the afternoon we changed into our home clothes before having just one lesson. How excited we all were. The coaches drew up ready to take us home. They all left in different directions as pupils came from far and wide. Our coach to Tunbridge Wells was the fastest coach. Not everyone went home in this way. Some travelled by train, taxi, bus or in their parents' car. As our coach got nearer to Tunbridge Wells I got more and more fidgety on my seat. At last we arrived outside the Assembly Hall. There were my parents waiting for me, as excited as I was. I talked and talked and told them all about my first week. How quickly the weekend went.

I soon settled into the rhythm of this new school but it was so very different from my last one. Because it was a boarding school and because it was for deaf children, far more outings, visits and clubs were arranged than for a day school. We had cub scouts, brownies and guides. Other children were allowed to join in local youth clubs with hearing children. There were discos and parties for those who enjoyed them. We were encouraged to have fund raising activities for other charities. We had a stream of visitors who talked to different classes on many different subjects. Older pupils from local schools sometimes came and helped. As far as possible the staff tried to give us a varied and rounded education. The spiritual side of life was not overlooked and various people who were used to speaking to the deaf came and spoke at assembly. Older children were also prepared for confirmation.

Sports are always popular in any school but with deaf pupils these energetic lessons are of even greater importance. Always trying to lip read, always trying to speak clearly can build up tensions in pupils. A good bout of football or running can disperse some of them.

At the end of my first year I had a good report. My language teacher was pleased with my flow of speech and my wide vocabulary but I was still finding it difficult to slow down sufficiently to make myself understood. I found this a problem for many years. Unfortunately it is the slurred and unintelligible speech of many deaf people which has given rise to the general public's reaction to them. Most people treat us as if we are not intelligent at all. Of course at school we had regular teaching on how to articulate all the sounds and words, but it is another thing to put it all into practice when you are feeling shy, or getting hot and bothered about something. All too easily speech gets sloppy.

On several occasions the headmaster enigmatically said in my report, 'Phillip has got into the kind of mischief that one would normally expect from a boy of his age.' Unfortunately as the years went by my behaviour became more and more unacceptable.

But before all the bad news, I did have my moments of glory. A regular visitor to our school was Dame Flora Robson. She had a special interest in deaf children and was very good to us. She frequently acted as narrator in our Christmas nativity play. When I was almost ten she came to make a film at our school to be shown on Christmas Day on BBC television. The National Deaf Children's Society had been given the peak day of the year to make their appeal. Filming took place in various areas of the school and showed us rehearsing our nativity play. The idea behind the film was partly to show how well we could do, but mainly to draw the heart strings of the viewers so that they would dip their hands into their pockets and send in donations. I was a loner very much of the time at school and as they were filming during a play time period they observed me leaning over a low wall, playing all on my own with a car. This appealed to the photographers and my lonesome figure was shown to thousands of viewers on Christmas Day.

Most children have a very strong sense of fair play and are quick to demand justice when authority strikes. Deaf children cannot always catch everything that a teacher says; neither can they express themselves accurately. As a result a sense of injustice can quickly grow. One day when I was twelve I was playing a really good war game with some friends. We were chasing each other and using our hands as guns to kill each other. I was the chief soldier and just as I was dashing across the gym, a young woman teacher who was really beautiful and who taught the youngest children in the school, walked in with a cup of coffee in her hand. As I dashed past her another soldier attacked me. I swung round and knocked her arm. The coffee splashed all over her clothes and mine. For obvious reasons, there was a strict rule that teachers were not allowed to carry drinks into the gym at any time, but this teacher was furious with me. She grabbed me and shook me. By now I was furious too. I hit her hard to let her know I was angry. I didn't want any teachers in the gym when we were playing our rough war games. I got into a wild temper. Other teachers soon arrived on the scene and caught me. I was shouting and crying. They pulled me harder and took me struggling to the library and told me to calm down. They told me I needed to rest there for a bit. I could smell all the coffee over my trousers, which were soaked. I sat around in the library for about an hour while a series of different teachers sat with me. I suppose they had to waste their free periods doing it. I thought of ways to escape but it was not possible.

By now the headmaster had been told about the fight and he sent for me in his office. I told him how it had begun, and what I had done. He sent for one of my friends to hear his version. My friend was very outspoken. He told the headmaster that it was the teacher who was in the wrong because she had not moved out of the way when we were in the middle of a war game and also that it was a clear rule that staff were not allowed to carry drinks around in the gym. The headmaster told my friend to leave the room. He hopefully asked if I could leave with him but the headmaster firmly said he wanted me to stay.

When we were alone he talked to me about fighting and breaking school rules and said he was going to ring up my father. 'What for?' I called out. If that teacher had not broken a rule, none of this would have happened. It sounded stupid to ring my father. I had not been in real trouble before and did not realise how serious my behaviour had been. All I felt was that the teacher and the headmaster were breaking rules. It was all very unfair. In spite of what I said, the headmaster phoned my dad. As he put the receiver down he said to me, 'Your father is coming straight away to fetch you. He'll take you home.'

'No!' I shouted. By this time the head was very angry with me.

'Yes, he is coming,' he said. I was so mad I got up and walked out of his office without saying another word. Two other tutors came up to me and told me to change out of school uniform and then to go and have tea with them. By the time I had done this I felt much calmer. I was allowed to play ball with some of the other children. About an hour later I was called indoors to the library. There stood my father. I began to cry. He told me not to worry and bundled me into the car and took me home. We were happy together. That all happened on a Thursday and I was not allowed to return to school until the following Monday.

I've said that sport is a good outlet for deaf children, but you can have too much of a good thing. There was one teacher in particular, Baggy, who kept us on the go the whole time. It was because I felt we never had a moment to ourselves that I got into so much trouble. Baggy was mad about football. He trained us very hard for the school team but we were never good enough for him. He wanted us to be the greatest team, but we couldn't possibly be. For a start we were a young team and then we were deaf, which does make a difference when playing with competitors who can hear instructions from the coach or encouraging cheers from the spectators. They can also hear if someone is coming up behind them.

Most of us wanted to play other games, not always football. Baggy was a good player himself but a bit of a show off. He could beat all of us in the gym, the playground or the fields alike.

There was one amusing time when we played football with a hopeless visiting team. After one of our players had scored eleven goals he was replaced by a weaker player to even things out. But we still scored goals. In the end the visiting team had all their players on the pitch against our seven. But we still beat them fifteen nil. How we laughed and laughed. They were the same age as us but just no good at football. They never played us again.

Apart from football Baggy did sometimes take us out for cross country runs. On one occasion he took us out from school in the mini-bus. It was cold and snowing in the late afternoon when we drove off. We went up into the Downs where we were dropped off not far from a race course. We had about four miles to run home. Soon it was too dark to see. We ran and ran keeping together, but two of the boys gradually ran ahead of us. The snow came down more heavily and their footprints were quickly covered up. We lost our way. The weather got worse and fog blew in from the sea to add to the snow. We stopped. We tried to find the right way but we were well and truly lost. We spread out in a line, one of us every few yards, down to the bottom of the hill to see where we were. The boy at the furthest end of the line said he could just see a number of houses, so we knew we'd come the wrong way. We all kept together and went up the hill to find the footpath.

We were beginning to get worried by now. We ran and walked, ran and walked for about a mile. Eventually we found that we were running along the race course itself. Suddenly through the snow we saw the headlights of a big car coming faster and faster over the grass. I shouted and waved my hands to the others to get them off the course as quickly as possible. I thought it must be a police car but it wasn't. The driver braked very hard and skidded through the grass. I was amazed to see it was the school mini-bus. In it was Baggy, angry as usual. He demanded to know what we were up to and why we had wasted so much time. I took the lead to answer him and explained how the other boys had run ahead too fast and that because of the snow we had not been able to keep them in sight. We told him we were sorry for the trouble, but please need we run in weather like this again? I expect Baggy's anger was partly worry and fear about what might have happened to us. Even he could now see the risks and said we would not go out again in such bad weather. He added that we would not get into trouble for getting lost. I should hope not! Oh! how I hated him at moments like this.

That was not the only time I got angry of course. One day at school I was feeling ill with a sore throat and a pain in my chest. It was lunch time and I was on my way to the dining-room. Before I got there I stopped by the wash basins. I knew that I could not eat any lunch that day. A teacher saw me there and told me to go into the dining-room. I turned away from her and she put her hand on me. I pushed her away and told her that I didn't want any dinner.

She quickly called some other members of staff. One of them asked me what the matter was. I did not answer and walked outside. The tutor thought that I was going to fight, and more teachers arrived. I shouted at them, 'Clear off! I don't want you!' I shoved them away and walked up and down. They rushed at me to grab me and I began hitting and kicking them as they jostled me into a small room by the wash basins. I held tightly on to the rows of shoe cubicles which covered one of the walls. By doing this, the teachers could not pull me down. Suddenly I had a good idea. Ammunition was at hand. I began to throw boots one after another down on to the staff. I wanted to let them know that I wanted to boot them off. I found I could throw with one hand and hold on tightly with the other. They pulled harder and harder to try to get me down but I managed to cling on.

By now more staff had arrived and one of them called a doctor. I went on fighting, kicking and punching. I hurt some of the teachers who retired from the battle. A strong group of them got me off the cubicles and tried to get me, as I struggled, to lie down on the floor. They walloped me to make me lie down. In the end I just lay there unable to move because so many of them were holding me down. Then to my horror they began to pull my trousers off. I immediately began to struggle wildly again, convinced that once my trousers were off I should get a beating with a stick. But that was not the reason. The doctor had arrived. He wanted to give me an injection in my bottom to calm me down. Very soon after he'd given it to me I felt very sleepy and weak. The staff had a good laugh when they saw me reduced to this state and they carried me unresisting upstairs to the sick bay, with my trousers safely back on. The doctor was amazed that I did not fall asleep immediately. I just felt tired. I was put to bed and sat up and watched television including *Play School* which came on after I'd had a quick sleep. When it was over I got out of bed and wandered into another room but some teachers were there keeping an eye on me and I could not escape.

I told them that I wanted to leave the sick bay, but they said that I looked too ill. I was not feeling ill by then, just very tired still. I went back to my bedroom and looked around. Something gave me an idea. I thought that I would take the mattress off the bed and throw it on the floor. I pulled it off, sheets and all and threw it down. Of course the staff heard the noise and came to the door. Quickly I moved the bed over to the door and rammed it shut. Now I was sure that no one could get in. Suddenly the door opened and there was the headmaster. I was amazed.

'What's wrong with you Phillip?' he asked.

He came into the room and talked to me, calming me down. He talked to the staff too and then went away. About an hour and a half later I had another visitor. My father! He took me down to the headmaster's study and left me there. The head tried to talk to me again and took out his stick and showed it to me. He was very nervous and I could see that his hands were shaking. He put it back on his desk. I knew that if he hit me I would hit him even harder. I knew that the headmaster knew that too. He was not a young man and had not been well. I walked out of his office and my father went in for a talk. The result was that I was sent home for about two and a half months.

I was bored at home even though my class teacher had set me some work. It was not much fun doing it on my own. My mother found that a teacher from the Kent Education Committee could come for several months to my home to teach me. He walked up from the centre of town and was a nice man. I liked him and he taught me well. I was able to lip read him. As it was the summer of the World Cup I got a game of table football called Subbuteo and my teacher sometimes played with me. As he only gave me lessons during the morning I was free every afternoon. I enjoyed this better than school. He taught me the best I've ever been taught. Looking back I realise that the deaf school was not the best.

One of the reasons I enjoyed being at home was that I felt part of the family again. While I had been away at boarding school, I had been given some news one day by the school matron. 'Your father has just phoned,' she said. 'Your mother has had a baby. A new brother for you.' I was quite pleased with the news but did not think much more about it until I returned home on Friday evening. Mum was not at home and my father cooked the tea. His meal was all right. Later in the evening, my father, Greg and I went to Pembury hospital to see my mother and the new baby. There were many other mothers sitting up in bed with their babies. We looked out for Mum and went to her bedside. The baby was asleep in a cot at the end of the bed.

I was intrigued to know what the colour of the baby's eyes were. Mum told me they were blue. I waited for him to open them, but he just went on sleeping. 'We're going to call him Colin,' Mum said. I was delighted. I had a friend called Colin and was able to say the word clearly. Later, as he opened his eyes I smiled at him. He looked nice. He had golden hair, quite different from all of us.

Colin was a good baby and I enjoyed seeing him at weekends. Because I was away he was given my bedroom and I slept with Greg in his room. One night I had a funny experience. Something went wrong. In the middle of the night I went out to the toilet. Afterwards as I was sleepy, I sleepwalked back into my old bedroom and got into bed. Everything felt funny. There was no bedstead and only one pillow. I felt around in the dark for my rabbit doll which I always took to bed with me. I shut my eyes and felt all over the inside of the bed and floor for it. Suddenly I woke up and was amazed to find I was in the wrong room. Colin woke up and saw me from his cot. I put him down to sleep but he began to cry. I ran off quickly back to Greg's bedroom and jumped into bed. In the morning I wondered if my parents would be cross with me, but nothing was said.

Now that I was home I could enjoy playing with Colin. He was almost two and fun to be with.

Just before the end of the summer term, I was allowed back to my boarding school. Sadly I said goodbye to my local teacher. It was a strange experience arriving once more for school. Perhaps because it was near the end of term we did not do much work. One day, a week before we broke up I got into trouble again. I was doing some football training with Baggy, but after about half an hour's work I was tired.

'Get a move on,' Baggy insisted. 'Work hard.' It was a hot July day, and all right for Baggy who just sat watching us do the job. I walked off.

Baggy rushed after me and said, 'Why won't you play?'

'I'm too tired and too hot,' I shouted.

'Say you're sorry!' he demanded.

'No. I hate you!' I cried. I walked out of the playing field and waited in the games room. Nobody was there and nobody came so I walked about, waiting. A teacher walked through and asked me if I was all right. I answered gruffly that I was, just about. I waited for what seemed another half an hour. The lessons must be long, I thought. All the time I was thinking of something to kill Baggy with, or at least to beat him. Then I stopped. I knew I could not kill him but when I saw him locking up the sports shed, I threw some stones at him.

He turned round and exclaimed, 'What on earth?!' My stones had not hit him so I threw more. Then he saw me. He picked some stones up and tossed them in my direction. I ran through the gates throwing more stones. Some boys got in the way and one was hurt on the leg. Baggy rushed to them and told them to get help quickly. I ran into the playground and got a long stick. Baggy immediately picked up a shorter one. I brought my stick up to nose level. I felt as if I was playing the dangerous Kendoka Japanese wooden sword game. Baggy did not know how to play it. I was stronger and taller than he was even though I was only thirteen. I moved my stick very quickly. It hit Baggy's stick which he now held in two hands over his head. I hit his stick harder and harder.

Suddenly a group of teachers and boys arrived. I was amazed that I was losing the fight and hit Baggy's stick again and again. Next I hit Baggy himself and hurt him. The staff rushed at me, and tried to catch me but I was wild and dangerous. Although I waved my stick about I didn't manage to land a blow. I got closer to one teacher and waving my stick lunged at him to hit him. All the teachers ran back. Just for a moment I lowered my stick and in a flash a teacher ran forwards and caught it. Too late. I was surrounded by teachers and pupils, just like in a football crowd. There was not a chance of escaping. I was grabbed firmly and led back to school.

'Get your bags and pack them. Go home and don't come back any more,' the headmaster said angrily to me. He gave me a letter for my father to tell him I had been expelled. I was put on the normal Friday afternoon coach and my father met me. When he told me that I could never return to the school I cried and cried.

'But I want to go back, I want to go back,' I kept saying all over the weekend. My father was trying to watch the British Grand Prix on the television, live from Brands Hatch. He got fed up with me interrupting him. I kept on and on about going back to school. In the end my father said, 'All right. All right. I'll give you a letter to the headmaster.' I felt happy again. On Sunday afternoon I waited for the school coach as usual but rather nervously in case anyone saw me and knew that I should not be there. The driver surely would not let me on. But he welcomed me aboard as usual.

'Passed!' I thought to myself. When the coach arrived back at school, I got out quietly, hiding my face and not looking at anyone. I hurried upstairs to my bedroom but some teachers had seen me from the sick bay and told the headmaster. I hid for a bit in the toilets and then came out. A tutor was waiting for me.

'Get your bag and your coat ready to . . .' he began, but I interrupted him and shouted,

'Wait! I've got a letter for the headmaster.' So the tutor told me to wait in the bedroom which I did nervously, wondering what would happen to me. After about fifteen minutes the tutor came back and handed me a letter.

'Get your coat and bag and go home,' he said.

I was sad. I'd failed to return to school. I walked down the hill with the tutor to the coach. He said I was to be allowed back for the last day or two of term only. I felt I just wanted a tank to blow the headmaster sky high. At the bottom of the hill the coach was still waiting for me. It had already started off but had been waved back to pick up the trouble-maker.

I sat in the middle of the empty coach, alone and sad. When I got back to Tunbridge Wells someone rang my father for me, to pick me up, but there was no reply. He told me to start walking home. Just at that moment my father arrived in his car but he did not see me. He gave a quick glance and drove off. I waved and waved to him but he still did not see me. I felt very sad and thought that by now he must hate me and that he did not want to give me a lift. So I walked home. As I got almost to the house, Greg saw me and called out to Dad, who came out to greet me and tell me he was sorry to have missed me down in the town. He took me indoors and said, 'Never mind about school. Forget all about that now.'

So it was all over. Deaf school had not done me much good. But it was good to be back as part of the family again. I did not know what my parents would plan for me. I would have to forget the old friends at school and make new ones here at home. It was a good thing the holidays were so close. We would all go away together. That would take my mind off everything.

6. Scouting Adventures

Soon I needed some outside activities. Not only did I need to meet and mix with other children of my age, it was essential that I had some outlet for my vitality. What better than the scouts? My parents made arrangements and I happily joined. The meetings were held in the church hall where once I'd attended Sunday school, so the setting was familiar. I went there every Tuesday. Sometimes Greg and I walked down there with our friends Alex and Dave from over the road. I put myself in charge of them, shouting, 'One, two, three, four, HALT!' It was a very funny way of getting there. 'Left, right, left, right, HALT! Right, left, right, left, HALT!' We all laughed but I was not sure whether the others were happy about it or not. It took much longer to get there of course. We always marched this wrong way, to the sweet shop first before we got to the hall. Sometimes we bought some chewing gum but mostly I bought wine gums. I loved them and ate them all myself. I did not want to share them. If someone came and asked me for a sweet I showed them my fist and said, 'I'll hit you if you want one.' So they rushed off. They were all frightened of me. I expect too that some of them had heard stories about why I'd had to leave my last school. I used to allow my patrol leader and some of my patrol a sweet. But sometimes I didn't give them one if they had been rude to me or had played me up. Boys from other patrols would complain and say 'It's not fair,' when I refused to give them sweets.

I enjoyed the rough and tumble games we played at scouts. Our leaders really got us to let off steam. Sometimes I got bored, because in the rush of each week's meetings the leaders did not always take my deafness into account and spoke too rapidly for me to lip read. No one thought of giving one scout the job of writing down important information for me, so I often missed out on knowing what was going to happen next – or next week, or next month. Looking back I can see it would have been sensible to have talked these problems over with Pawly the leader but at thirteen I just felt frustrated and that nobody cared.

Pawly and Stone were the two men in charge of us. Both of them were heavily-built rugger types, weighing about fourteen to eighteen stone. They were ideal to be in charge of us rabble! My favourite game we played was British Bulldog. This is an energetic wrestling game guaranteed to wear us out and strengthen our muscles. In it, one scout is chosen to be the British bulldog. The rest of us line up facing him at the far end of the hall. We have to run past him to the other end. The bulldog has to catch someone and grab him firmly enough to pick him up. This new scout now joins the bulldog in catching others, and so on until we are all caught. On one occasion I noticed that the bulldog was a very thin boy. Far too thin to pick me up, let alone Pawly who was also playing that night. Gradually, the other boys were caught but I ran harder and harder and was the last to be grabbed. Last except for Pawly. He had taken his shirt off to make it harder for us to hold on to him. He ran fast to the other line. I ran to catch him but missed him. The other scouts were too scared to tackle him. I chased him again, even though I only weighed ten stone. All the other scouts were cheering me on, and at last I managed to catch him with my left hand around his shoulders. All the bulldogs rushed at him and finally we lifted him up. That was a great victory for all of us, but also for me, catching him first. I was too strong for him in the end. Sometimes he got fed up with me.

One day as we were preparing to go home, I noticed that someone had taken the leather rig off my scout scarf. I tried to find out who had got it and finally retrieved it. To teach them a lesson I rushed at the boys who'd done it and tossed their caps off their heads, refusing to give them back. Finally their dad arrived, a large, fat, wealthy man. By now the boys had taken Greg's rig. Their dad got cross with me, and Dave told me I must give the hats back. 'You're always causing trouble,' their dad said. I tossed the caps back to them and without warning, turned and walked home.

One of the features of scout life was the annual camp. I looked forward to this and enjoyed it, though as usual such an event did not pass without incident. When I went, I dressed smartly in uniform, as requested. I was surprised to see that some scouts arrived looking quite dirty and scruffy. Before we left, we all met together in the church hall while we were waiting for the removal lorry to arrive to take us off to camp. When it drew up we hurried out with our gear and packed it carefully, loading our tents and cooking equipment first. Next came our personal luggage, rucksacks and cases. We made sure to leave a bit of space for us. Then we returned to the hall and marched into a line for the final parade before we set off. Terry Southam said prayers for the coming camp. We could hardly wait to get in the lorry and rushed off the moment he'd finished.

The field for our camp near Hailsham had recently been an orchard. The old trees had been bulldozed away leaving a very rough and lumpy area for us. We all jumped out of the lorry and formed a long chain to unload the gear as quickly as possible. The first thing to do was to put up our tents to keep everything dry in case it rained.

We were kept very busy on these camps although there were the usual times when I felt left out.

The most memorable day was when we played what is known as a wide game. This took a whole day and was meant for fun, for training and for tiring us out! We had to walk about twenty-six miles across country, through villages and along lanes to find map references, names of people on notice boards, times of church services and other bits of information. We also had to find various stickers which had been hidden along the route the night before by the leaders.

We left camp at about nine in the morning, divided into groups. I was in the Stags. My friend Dave, and John who did the same paper round as me were in the Stags too. There were also some other good scouts in our group so we stood a chance of doing well. Each of us carried our own packed lunch and one of us carried a rucksack with maps and our macs and cagoules in case it rained. We were the lightest group, carrying very little. We could see that the other groups were too heavily laden to run very easily. We did well finding stickers and working out the map references and finding the shortest way between each point.

When we were about ten miles from camp we met one of the other groups. They couldn't find the next sticker. We knew where it might be, and that they had probably passed it only a few yards behind them. We said, 'Bye' to them casually and in about twenty seconds had found the sticker for ourselves, hidden on the back of a milestone. We plodded on and finally got back into camp at about eight o'clock in the evening. We were the first group back and had won the game. All our points were added up for each day and at the end of the week the Stags were leading.

Nearly everything we did in camp helped us gain experience in the skills needed for the scout standard badge, a difficult badge to gain. The wide game with its map reading and following instructions was an important part of the test. So were the camp skills of pitching tents, making equipment, keeping camp orderly, keeping tools safe and knowing how to use them, knotting, lighting fires etc. It was a great occasion when I finally passed all the various tests and was presented with the badge. Terry Southam gave the scouts a talk about how hard I'd had to work to gain this badge and how I'd done it in spite of being deaf. Terry often spoke up for me in difficult times and tried to help the other boys think about the problems of being deaf. But in rough and tumble games you cannot always expect a group of boys to think of that.

We did various other badge work too at camp and this all gained our teams extra marks, more than if we'd just stayed at home in the scout hut in Tunbridge Wells. I was very keen for the Stags to win the highest score, so I was always very quiet at night and kept our tent quiet, so that we would not lose points. Also I cleaned the tents well for extra marks. I was cook for the week for the Stags which I enjoyed. Others helped me peel the potatoes.

One thing used to annoy me. We all brought our own cutlery to camp, marked with our names. When other scouts laid the tables they did not care how they did it. They laid out the cutlery all mixed up so that every boy got a mixture of other boys' cutlery. I thought this was awful. Whenever possible I would go round and sort it all out, so that we each ate with our own cutlery. I tried to get the others to do the same but they did not take any notice of me.

There was a real trouble-maker at camp. I shall call him Goose. He was always up to tricks. One day when Stone was driving out of the field to fetch water in the big tanks Goose climbed on to the roof rack and held on. Stone was going bumpily over the field. He put his arm out of the window and held on to Goose to stop him from falling off. There could have been a nasty accident if Goose had fallen off in front of the car, once it got on to the road. Goose was always a trouble-maker, just like me!

One night I got into a bit of trouble myself. I cannot remember the details but Pawly got cross with me and told me to move into the other tent to sleep with him. I refused to go. Pawly tried to get me into the other tent, but I became violent with him and tackled him, knocking him to the ground. From this position Pawly gave me a piece of his mind and told Stone I was to sleep in his tent. Still I refused and challenged anyone else to a fight. Headly, my patrol leader, who understood me very well, persuaded Pawly that I would behave back in the tent if I were given another chance. So I was allowed to remain in my tent, though Stone joined us as a supervisor. Poor Headly, being a good leader, slept in Pawly's tent, to make room for Stone.

On the last day of camp we had a sports day. The Stags won the 1979 Camp Games Award. We had great fun during races calling out to the other teams, 'Come on lazy bones.' So the camp ended on a high note of enjoyment and achievement.

Apart from the annual week's camp we also had the occasional weekend camp. At one of these one of the rather thick scouts brought a pile of girlie magazines with him. He made sure to hide them from the two leaders, but in the morning they were found and confiscated. During lights out that night we all played about and made a lot of noise. No one came to tell us off. Where could the leaders be? We got noisier and noisier. We thought the leaders must be busy reading the confiscated magazines. Now I should imagine they were down at the pub having a quick drink!

On normal weekday scout meetings we sometimes went up on to Tunbridge Wells Common for games. It is an ideal place with rocks, woods, bracken and open spaces. One of the favourite games we played up there was a chasing and catching game with plenty of opportunities for scuffles. On one occasion I was tackled by the infamous Goose, and in the tussle he hit my hearing aid. It fell to the ground and broke. Fortunately the hospital was quite used to teenage boys' hearing aids getting damaged. It was replaced by them and no one had to pay, though as my dad explained we all help to pay through our taxes.

Another game I enjoyed at scouts was a racing game, Sedan Chairs. First of all we put two long sticks across a chair and roped them on securely to make it into the sedan chair. We had to do this strongly so that it was safe enough to carry one of the scouts. Then the race began. We put the lightest boy from our patrol into the chair, lifted him up and took him up to the park at the back of the hall, ran right round it and finally, exhausted, returned to the hall. One of the teams made the mistake of putting a very heavy boy into their chair and so no one could lift it up. While we were rushing round the park we sometimes lost our balance and dropped the poor scout out of the chair.

Gradually I decided that I'd had enough of scouts, but once I'd left I wondered whether I'd like to meet up with them again, so later I rejoined, but this time in the Venture Scouts. Again Goose was there, getting into trouble. Unfortunately I found the Venture Scouts boring. I found there was nothing to do that interested me and once again I made a nuisance of myself. For example on one evening we were having a dancing lesson (Venture Scouts had boys and girls). I was not keen to join in. Although I could not hear the music I could pick up the vibrations, but it did not appeal to me. I wanted to do something more interesting. So I pulled all the wires out from the plug and no sound came out. Every one stopped dancing and looked around. The teacher in charge was very cross with me because I kept stopping the music. Later that evening, I got violent with my leader and we were just ready for a fight. But in a way it was not his fault. He had no insight into the sheer frustration of being deaf. Once again Terry Southam came to the rescue. 'After all,' he said, 'it's not his fault he's deaf.'

By now I was busier with my church youth group and found the activities more to my liking, so I drifted away from scouts altogether.

Years later I saw my old scout leader again. He was riding his bike. I saw that he had lost a lot of weight and was quite thin. I also saw that he was riding an old bike which could not go very fast. I was on my racer at the time, on the way home from visiting someone. I followed him for a long distance, very slowly. I could see that he was much older now. Up and down the hills I followed him. He seemed to get slower and slower and I felt quite worried. I couldn't bring myself to pass him. In the end, he went so slowly I thought to myself, 'Take no notice,' then I rode faster and faster and finally overtook him. As I passed him I didn't dare to look at him. I sped on faster and faster round three corners. Then I looked back, but he was not in sight. 'Poor old Pawly,' I thought as I saw him riding so slowly, and his having lost so much weight. His only memory of me must surely be of trouble.

Another interest I had at this time was table tennis. Dave my friend and I joined a weekly table tennis club. It was held down in the same hall as scouts. Greg and Alex came occasionally. I always associate that hall with trouble because I used to get mad at scouts and mad at table tennis! Sometimes I shouted and threw bats, because I was not playing well. I used to hit the ball too hard and very rarely won. The other players were nervous of me and brought up chairs to the table to protect themselves from my vicious playing. One time we all played with matches in the kitchen at the back of the hall, and burned some table tennis balls. 'Surely,' I thought, 'someone will smell the flames?' but no one came. What a risk we were taking with fire. Sometimes they were three star tennis balls and quite expensive. Once I broke a boy's table tennis bat and refused to buy another one for him. The leader contacted my father and told him what I'd done. My father, naturally, was cross with me. He bought a new bat to replace the broken one and made me pay him back a small amount every week.

By now I had joined a large school in a nearby town. I was doing well in sports there, and these activities were able to absorb some of my energies and frustrations.

7. Beginnings of My Christian Life

During my years at boarding school I had been coming home every weekend and going to church on Sundays with my family. Slowly, bit by bit, I was learning about the Bible and Jesus. But I was not learning much. I missed most of what was read and taught. I could only lip read occasional phrases when the Bible was being read and much of what the Sunday school teacher said to me was lost. The leaders seldom spoke to me personally as it was too hard for them to get me to understand what they were saying. They did not take their opportunity to teach me clearly about Jesus, and left it too late. I wonder sometimes why this was. If I had known more words and teaching from the Bible perhaps my life at boarding school might not have been so terrible.

As I grew older I did not go as regularly as I once had. When I had been at home from boarding school for a couple of months my father said to me one Sunday that I was to get ready for church.

'I'm not coming. It's so boring,' I said. To my surprise my father explained that we were going to visit a new church, quite different from the Anglican church we'd been attending.

'The services are more lively. There will be more going on for you to see,' Dad said. We left home earlier than usual at about half past nine.

We arrived at an old building in the centre of town. Judging by the outside appearance I could imagine how grubby and neglected it would look like on the inside. I had a big surprise. Everything was clean and attractive and there were beautiful bright colours on the walls. The building itself was old and was due to be sold as it was structurally unsound in parts. It would cost too much for a congregation to repair. Meanwhile it had temporarily been rented to the Central Pentecostal Church, who had transformed its interior.

Everything inside that church was different from anything I'd met before. To begin with when Dad had met the pastor and had a chat with him, he came over to me and warmly shook my hand. No vicar had ever done that. I was surprised. I did not realise who he was, and I was still looking round for someone who looked like a vicar with a cassock and a dog collar. I could not see anyone like that anywhere. My mother explained that in this church the leader was called a pastor and did not wear any special clothes. The man who had shaken hands with me had been wearing an ordinary suit and tie.

As we were so early not many people had arrived but gradually more and more came and the service started with music. The pastor stood behind a small pulpit up on the platform with members of the congregation who were playing in the music group. This consisted of a piano, an electric organ and a violin. This was played by an elderly man who jigged around, playing without any music. He must have been playing for a long time to be able to do that.

When other children left the service to go into Sunday school, someone came up and spoke to me. My father quickly explained that I was deaf and told him how old I was. The leader was surprised that I was only thirteen as he had imagined I was much older. This surprised me. My father arranged for me to join the Sunday school after Christmas.

Everything in the service was strange and I could not understand what was going on. I'd never seen the custom of lifting up arms and hands while people were singing or praying. My mother explained that it was a happy and joyful response to God, a desire to praise him and worship him. I thought it was quite a good service and better than the Church of England. So we began going there regularly and I joined the youth group.

To begin with I found it hard to settle into the youth group because like young people everywhere they laughed and joked between themselves and spoke very rapidly, rarely remembering to slow down for me, or even to face me properly when speaking to me. Once again during their Bible studies I got bored. I just sat on the end of the bench and could not follow what was happening.

There was one boy who tried to make friends, Adrian Pope. He came and told me about himself and about his being blind in one eye. He wrote some words and sentences down on paper for me. The leader of the youth group suddenly realised how much I had been missing. He asked Adrian to write down notes for me in Bible studies, and any notices that were given out. This was a great help. I began to feel part of the group. For the first time I began to receive regular Christian teaching.

Gradually as I learned more about the Bible my heart warmed towards Jesus. People often asked me when exactly I became a Christian. That is a very hard question to answer. I think it began at this time. I did want to follow Jesus but I did not understand all that that involved. I led a double life in a way. Part of me belonged to Jesus and part of me went my own way. Everything is much clearer now and I am completely committed to Christ. I know that I believe Jesus, I believe God and I believe the Holy Spirit and all the Bible. But when I was fourteen I was not sure what I believed.

During church services I tried to pray and worship the Lord well. I was not very good at singing because I could not hear the tune or know how fast everyone was going. As the music group expanded over the years to include drums I was able to feel the vibrations of the rhythm. In fact I enjoyed playing the drums myself and it was fun to feel part of the service in this way.

One day when I was fourteen the pastor talked about being baptised into the body of Christ. In the Pentecostal

Church babies are not baptised by sprinkling water on them. They are brought into the service and dedicated to God. Later, when a person has become a Christian and wants to follow Jesus he or she asks for believer's baptism, which takes place during a service. In it the believer is plunged beneath the water in a small baptismal pool which is concealed under the floor at the front of the church. I had seen various people being baptised by immersion in this way.

I thought about what the pastor had said and told my mother that I wanted to be baptised myself. She explained it to me and we went to see the pastor. He knew me well and had watched me settle into the church and had seen my faith grow. He said I was to come to a class for baptismal candidates. I went with my mother. There were not many people there. The pastor spoke too quickly for me, and my mother noticed me looking round the room. She touched me with her hand and said, 'Try and listen. We'll see him again afterwards to find out what he says.' When the meeting was over we went and talked to the pastor on our own, and he explained again simply about baptism. He did not say too much in case I should not follow him. When I spoke to him, he found it hard to understand me.

We went home and talked about it again. Mum told me that the service was to be the following Sunday evening. It was to be the last baptismal service in the old church as the lease had run out.

At last Sunday came. I felt quite excited and a little nervous. The church was packed and the atmosphere full of expectancy. Most people felt sad to be leaving the building. I was wearing a white shirt and my school trousers. My family and various friends sat in the front pew with me. Other baptismal candidates sat nearby with their relations.

The orchestra was in full strength and playing vigorously. I could feel the rhythm and vibration of the drums. The singing was loud and joyful. Then the time came for the baptisms. The pastor spoke for a while to the congregation telling them the meaning of baptism and how it was for believers. 'Being baptised will not make you into a Christian,' he said, 'it is a sign that you already are one.' Then he explained how baptism is a picture or symbol of death and resurrection. 'We were therefore buried with him through baptism into death in order that, just as Christ was raised from the dead through the glory of the Father, we too may live a new life' (Romans 6:4).

The first person went forward. I watched very carefully to see exactly what I should do. The pastor spoke to the candidate with a microphone in his hand and asked him questions about his faith. Then he and another pastor went down into the water. The candidate followed and was baptised. I thought to myself that when my turn came I would try to speak out clearly.

Someone gave me a signal and I was next. My family and friends left their seats and crowded round to see better. The pastor told the congregation that I was totally deaf. I could not hear a word spoken to me but I could hear God, who had spoken to me and I was obeying his call to baptism. Everyone was listening intently. Next the pastor asked me a question, but he spoke too quickly as he handed the mike to me. I just looked at it quite speechless. The pastor tried again but I could not lip read him. Then I spotted my father. Slowly he mouthed the words that the pastor had spoken.

'Do you love Jesus?'

I could understand that question. I spoke out loudly.

'Yes,' I said. The pastor was happy and smiled and repeated my answer to the whole congregation. There were some people in tears to think that Jesus could speak to me even though I was deaf. Then the two pastors placed their hands on my head and prayed for me. I prayed too.

'I love you Jesus,' I said. All this time I had been standing with my feet in the water, which was warm, but my trousers clung to me and felt funny.

After the prayer the pastor led me down into the water and vigorously dipped me under it with a prayer. I came up, water streaming from my hair and face. I was now baptised into the body of Christ, but apart from feeling very wet, I did not feel any other emotion. My mother had chosen some special music to be played at this moment, but of course I could not hear it. Someone covered me with a large towel as I clambered up the steps and I went into the changing room.

While I was drying myself my father stood waiting, beaming all over his face. What a day for him that his eldest son had been baptised. Then we went back into the church and although I could not hear the music I could sense the atmosphere and I was full of joy.

I praise God that gradually my life changed. I learned more about the Bible and the meaning of sin. I found many of the words in the Bible hard to understand. A modern translation was a great help, because like all deaf people my vocabulary is limited and every new word gained is something to treasure. Hearing people become familiar with words used over and over again in different contexts. Gradually they build up a broad picture of the word and its various meanings. A deaf person does not have that constant background of repetition. Therefore unusual words in the Bible which are not part of everyday speech anyway, take a good deal of study to understand.

Nowadays if I do not understand some words from the Bible I don't mind asking other Christians to explain the meaning to me. Also in the past my father used to spend a lot of time going over verses in the Bible with me and teaching me important truths. I use dictionaries frequently, but these are not always accurate about Bible words. I have read all through the books in the New Testament and a good deal of the Old Testament. I carry on regularly reading. I'm not waiting until I get to heaven to learn all I can about Christ. I want to learn now. My advice to anyone reading this is to keep on reading the Bible. Don't say 'I know, I know,' to yourself. That will be sinning if you think you know everything and do not need to hear what God says about your life.

For all of us life goes on at many different levels and the

slow growth of my Christian faith was mixed up with all the usual interests, fears and anxieties of any teenager. Sometimes I got very muddled. I would want to tell someone about Jesus and when they didn't want to listen I would punch them on the nose! I think I've learned better now!

Sport as I tell in a later chapter was very important to me. I think cricket was my first love at this time. I was not very good at it and needed more practice in the nets at school. Unfortunately school was too far away for me to stay late or to go to during the evenings. I asked a teacher if he knew which club I could join in my area. He told me I could practise at the Tunbridge Wells Cricket Club and that I could join the Colts. I thanked him for his advice and decided to join. I went along one Friday evening to the cricket ground. I found to my surprise that it was only five minutes' walk away from home, hidden away down a little lane. It is in fact the ground where county matches are played. I waited around a bit, too shy to speak to anyone. I saw some other young boys arrive and I watched them practise. I could still not summon up enough courage to ask if I could join in. At last a man came over to me and asked if I wanted to practise. I said that I did. My chance had come. I worked hard and practised and practised, but I was no good at all. I went there every Friday until the end of July but I did not understand how to practise properly. I found it difficult and I needed much more time to improve.

About this time I took up photography, a hobby I enjoyed very much. To begin with I had a cheap Russian camera which used a 35 mm film. Later I bought a flash gun. I enjoyed taking pictures of anything that took my fancy until I saw the results and realised how expensive photography was. After that I was more careful. Now I like to think carefully about a picture, make sure it is going to be good and that I'm taking it at the right speed. I took some interesting pictures of important buildings in and around Tonbridge for my CSE history exam. I enjoy taking close up pictures of flowers and have found that a slow speed is good for that as well as for landscapes and mountains.

I've sold my first camera and bought a much better one with a 100–200 mm zoom lens. I also use filters now and a tripod. I have all the expensive gear but I have to admit that my pictures are not much better than before.

Holidays are important to everyone, but especially when you are deaf. The steady concentration of lip reading and trying to speak clearly can become very exhausting and a break in routine and fresh things to see can help you to unwind. The new church we were going to made a great feature of church holidays especially for the young people and the summer after my baptism I had my first taste of camping in Wales, about twelve miles from Snowdon. We went as a family and drove all the way there, arriving early in the morning at about six o'clock. The camp was well laid out with rows of bell tents, all with electric lighting. My father was in charge of various things in the camp and I went round with him to find the mains switches, for turning the lights on and off at night. By lunch time Pastor Moye and his family arrived. He and his son Alan took me in their van to collect the gas canisters for the week's cooking.

But I had something else on my mind. Back on St Valentine's day I had received a card. My first ever. And I was not sure who it was from, but I had my ideas. I thought it was from one of the girls who had come on the holiday. I thought that if I chatted her up I might find out. So the next day I went to one of the girls' tents and met two of the girls, and each said the other might be my girlfriend. I was no nearer to guessing who had sent me the card. The girl I liked best out of the two went off with another boy for the rest of the week so I felt miserable and unhappy.

As it was a church holiday we had services every evening. More hours for me to feel isolated. More hours for me to sit as part of a crowd but completely cut off from what was going on. I was on holiday. I wanted to be free to play and do what I liked. We did go off for outings, like fishing and climbing Snowdon, but my memories of that camp are not happy ones.

So my family and I left camp for our own holiday in

Devon. I expect I was still feeling disgruntled after camp because I was soon having a fight with Greg. In the fight we broke my little brother Colin's new tractor. My father was very angry with us and we were not able to replace it with a new one.

When we finally got home from holiday my parents were still upset. I don't know all the reasons. They were not finding the new church as suitable for them as they had at the beginning.

I was still muddled in my Christian life. Part of me wanted to think about girls and how to get a girlfriend. My youth leader gave me a book called *The Little White Book*. I took it home and read it carefully. It helped me to make up my mind to be a better Christian. I was determined to follow Christ wholeheartedly. I decided to give up thinking about girls, but this was not easy, especially at school.

By Christmas my parents and brother had decided to leave the church and to join one in London. I knew that I would stay on with the local church where I had learned a lot and where my friends were. Once my parents had left I felt very much alone again, as they had often helped me during services. I had to rely on the young people more. I had not been well for some time so when I returned they all crowded round me and welcomed me. I was glad of that because I was upset that my parents had moved to another church. It upset me too that they did not like the one I felt so happy in. I do not know all the reasons as to why they moved, and anyway their reasons are private to them, but perhaps it was too hard for them to settle in one place. They had moved many times before.

I went with them once up to their London church but I did not want to go there regularly. For one thing I thought about all the fuel my father would use on the journey. It was about thirty-two miles away.

So the year in which I began my Christian life was fairly mixed with the joyful moments of my baptism tempered by failures of behaviour on my part and sadness in our family. But the Christian life always is a mixture like that.

8. Another Attempt at School

I had been expelled. So what were my parents to do with me now? I think we all felt cautious about tackling another school immediately. I was just pleased to be back as part of the family and relieved not to be chased around so much by Baggy. But this could not go on for long. Once again my parents, through the KCC, arranged for me to have a home tutor, but having my lessons day after day at home was not very stimulating. Later in the term I travelled across the town to a teaching centre and had my lessons there. Naturally my parents were anxious that I should get back into proper schooling as soon as possible.

Life at home was much calmer and I began to feel more settled. My mother began to make enquiries about suitable local schools. One day, near the end of the autumn term, she came in looking quite excited. She'd heard of a secondary school, Hugh Christie, in Tonbridge which had a partially hearing department for about thirty pupils. The school itself was large with about sixteen hundred pupils. Perhaps it would be a good idea for me to join a hearing school as a day boy with lessons in the PHD? The prospect was at least worth investigating. We set out for an interview. The school was modern with light, airy classrooms, set in large playing fields with trees and country views. I liked the look of it.

After the enclosed feeling of a boarding school which was entirely for deaf children, everything was different here.

'We like every child who has a hearing disability to spend as much time as possible in the main school, with hearing pupils,' Mr Harding the head of the PHD explained.

'You mean they don't have all their lessons here?' Mum asked, looking round the friendly huts which were used for the PHD.

'No. Every child is on the roll of one of the school house groups. They meet together every day. As a member of this mixed ability group Phillip will be a full member of the school, rather than just belonging to the PHD. After the daily group period Phillip will join classes suitable for his attainment and potential ability.'

'That sounds all right,' said Mum, 'but what about speech therapy, and extra help with lip reading and things like that?'

'Every day Phillip will have certain lessons here in the PHD. The amount of time will depend on his needs. As Phillip is totally deaf, which is unusual for us, as most of our pupils have a degree of hearing, he may only join the main school for practical lessons like art, pottery, and sport. But he will be first and foremost a full pupil of Hugh Christie School and a member of the PHD after that.'

I found it hard to follow everything that Mr Harding was saying. He smiled at me and I had a little interview with him. I felt dismayed that I could not understand him and decided my last school had not taught me too well! I also met two other teachers, one of whom, Mr Sharpe, I was to get to know very well. The headmaster, Mr Howard, came over to the PHD. He must have known all about me and why I had had to leave my old school, but he asked me to join the school. I thought about it carefully. Then both Mr Harding and Mr Howard said, 'Yes, come on, Phillip, do!'

I smiled at them and answered 'Yes'.

Perhaps it would be all right. They told me that they would expect to see me the following Monday for the last week of term before the Christmas holidays. So, I was back in school again. My father took me by car, very early on my first day, and I was given a bus pass. I was to stay at school for the mornings only.

I felt very strange as I went into the classroom for my first group period. There were about thirty-two pupils all much older than me. After this I went back to the PHD and met a new teacher who had come specially for me. Her name was Mrs Edwards. I spoke to her and found that she could understand me very well. I was pleased, but puzzled, because most people found it difficult to understand my speech. I asked her about this and how it was that she could understand me. She just said that my speech was clear to her. What pleased me as well was that I could lip read her easily, although she spoke quite rapidly. There was something about the way she shaped her lips which made her easy to follow. I was sure she must be a specially trained teacher for the deaf, but apparently she had had no extra experience.

The day began with a maths lesson which went on for about an hour. I was glad to be back in a school atmosphere again and settled down to work hard. There was so much I wanted to learn, so much I wanted to find out. I asked Mrs Edwards many questions and she always gave me very clear explanations. At some point I was given tests to do and they discovered that I was really very intelligent. The teachers knew then that I could work well if I chose to. I found the new work harder and more demanding than in my other school. It was a challenge and I felt rather like a sponge, sucking up everything I could learn.

Some boys whom I'd known years ago at my very first school, Slade, had heard I was there and at lunch time they came to the PHD and waited for me. They took me off and showed me the way to the hall and how to get our dinner. I found the large crowds rather overwhelming. Seeing so many other children frightened me, especially as I was wearing my school uniform from my last school and looked very different from everyone else. Mr Harding, our group tutor, had told me that if anyone in the school was rude to me or tried to have a punch, I was to let him know and he would pull their ears and speak to them! After lunch my friend Paul Skinner took me to the bus stop to go home.

While I was on the bus I looked out of the windows at everything we passed. I had enjoyed my first half-day and told my father all about it when he met me in Tunbridge Wells.

I was pleased at the beginning of the next term to be wearing the correct school uniform. I no longer looked any different from other children, except I wore a hearing aid. In my case I used a body-worn aid. This is larger than the coventional aid worn behind the ear, and is worn pinned on the front of a shirt or sweater, or slung round the neck or secured in a pocket. The body-worn aid gives greater magnification of sound. My teachers were able to make use of my minimal hearing to teach me rhythms of speech and they are sure that without my aid, I would not be able to speak as clearly as I do now.

I hated wearing the aid and often tried to leave it off. Wearing it showed both helpful and unhelpful pupils that I was deaf. The unhelpful ones teased me and were rude. But in this school there were also helpful pupils. The whole school was taught how to deal with deaf people, and shown how to face them and to speak clearly. Every new intake of pupils was told about the PHD and given an amusing questionnaire to fill in to help them come to grips with the deaf in their midst. The teaching staff too when they arrived for the first time were invited to visit the PHD to discuss how best to help deaf pupils and how much liaison there was between teachers in the PHD and staff in the rest of the school. Every teacher is given at the beginning of the year a list of all the deaf children, with notes about their degrees of deafness, where they should sit in the classroom, and how much lip reading each needs to do. If any teacher finds it hard to communicate with a particular child, or finds that extra work is needed to be done to consolidate a lesson, he can discuss this with a teacher in the PHD and get the problem sorted out. This seems a very good system and better than being away in a school entirely for the deaf. A school like this offers the best of both worlds. It enables the deaf child to be part of a normal school and to mix freely with hearing pupils, an essential preparation for going out to work later. It also offers regular speech training and extra tuition in basic subjects.

To begin with I had most of my lessons in the PHD. I had so much catching up to do. But I did have PE and pottery over in the hearing school. I was very nervous in these classes as they were fifth year pupils and I was only a third year. Although I was very tall for my age, so I did not look out of place, I felt it. However much a school tries to train the rest of the pupils how to approach other deaf pupils, there will always be some children who deliberately set out to aggravate them. And we deaf pupils are not perfect. I often got into fights which I suppose is normal teenage behaviour for boys. Once I was playing five-a-side football. One boy tried to knock me down all through the game. So I hit him harder and knocked him down. No one was able to catch me up. I shouted to the PE teacher for help. After this lesson I reported the incident to Mr Harding and he spoke to the boy concerned.

I also got into trouble in pottery because the boys were rude to me, mimicking me and deliberately speaking too fast. Very often they cracked jokes and laughed and of course I thought they were laughing at me. I expect they were just normal schoolboy jokes, but I felt very isolated. These feelings made me angry inside. When one of the boys was rude to me I grabbed him and lifted him up. The teacher was nervous and afraid that I might throw the boy down roughly and so he reported me to Mr Harding and it was my turn to be told off.

Pottery was a good lesson to get rid of some of my frustrations. I remember one day feeling really mad in a pottery lesson. I was on the electric wheel, making a bowl. In my other school I'd been used to the kick wheels. This electric wheel took me by surprise. I put my foot on the pedal and pushed it down for full speed. The clay whirled round and shot off the wheel. My clay was too wet and everything smashed up. I tried to mould this bowl for about three minutes until the teacher rushed up to me and told me not to push the pedal down so much. I was very embarrassed and said, 'Oh, sorry.' When he went away I smelled smoke from the machine. I knew that I'd burned the engine, so I took my clay off and went over to the kick wheel. I felt safer there. That day I was not successful. My bowl was a complete mess.

By the following autumn term, I was ready to join more classes in the main school as well as having a wider range of lessons in the PHD. Now I was at school for the full day. No more holiday atmosphere of half-days. The subjects I was taking were human biology, which fascinated me, particularly genetics, maths, English, history, geography, technical drawing, PE, art design, art general and woodwork. For the first few months I worked hard and did not find the extra work too much. Gradually Mr Harding noticed that I was very tired and not working very well. This was because I'd begun a paper round and was getting up at six in the morning. After a bit of persuasion by my father I let my brother Greg take over the round. Immediately my school work improved.

I was very mixed up at this time. I'd become a Christian and was preparing to be baptised, but because of my poor speech I could not tell other people about Jesus. This upset me.

I wanted to tell some of the rough, rude boys at school about Jesus because I thought if they knew him it would change them. As it was I could not explain clearly and they did not want to listen and I got very angry. When they made rude gestures to me and swore I would catch them later in the day. I'd make them show me the fingers they'd gestured with. Then I bent them back and they ran off with their fingers hurting. Now I think about it I did not use the best evangelistic methods!

Because I was travelling back at normal schooltimes on the busy school buses I had more opportunity to fight and get into trouble.

One of my best friends whom I'd known years before at the Slade school, Jonathan Bird, travelled with me. On one occasion I got very angry with him and we had a fight. I held his coat and banged his head against a telephone box. One of my teachers was very cross with me. So Jonathan and I made it up and we became friends again. But that did not stop our fights. At the bus stop when we were on the way home I had another fight. A police woman came up to me and told me to stop and to behave myself. She did not know that I was deaf and that I had not understood everything she'd said. I answered her, 'No, I might want to fight you.' She said that she would call up the police station on her radio and that I might go to jail and that I would not like that. So I stopped fighting and became friends again with Jonathan, and it never happened again.

All boys have fights like that naturally. But once on the bus journey I got into serious trouble. It began with a bit of fun. I locked up a boy's school bag and hid his keys in my bag. When it was nearly time for the boy to get off he asked me for the keys back. I said, 'Yes,' but horrors! I couldn't find the keys. I got very worried and the bus stopped. Jonathan said to me that we must both get out. So I rushed downstairs but I still could not find them. I ran to the back of the bus, because I did not want to get off the bus a long way from home. Someone told the driver what was happening. He got out of his seat and walked down the bus to me.

'Get out and wait for the next bus, then you can find the keys,' he shouted. I rushed past him shouting rudely on the way. When I got to the front of the bus I pushed the gear lever into first gear. The whole bus began to judder. I jumped quickly off the bus and closed the doors by pressing the switch on the outside. The driver hurried back to the front and tried to put the gears back into neutral. I was still outside, looking for the keys. The driver was also trying to open the doors. Finally he managed it by using some special controls. He was cross about the damage and all the waste of time. He jumped out of the bus and nearly caught me.

At that moment I pulled my hand out of my bag. 'I've found them,' I said. The driver stopped chasing me.

'Now you've found them I want you both to come to the

bus station about this trouble.' He grabbed Jonathan and me and hauled us back on to the bus. I saw everyone watching us wide-eyed on the bus, but they didn't say anything. We finally drove off and when we got to Tunbridge Wells the driver took us into the bus station to write his report.

When I got home I told my mother all about it. She was upset and told me I must never behave like that again. She thought that the bus company would report the incident to Hugh Christie School. The next morning I went in very sheepishly, but not a word was said. I don't know why the bus company did not complain.

Various other fights and adventures on the buses soon singled me out as the strongest boy on the bus. Fortunately at this time I became very keen on sport at school and it was this outlet for my energy which perhaps prevented me from getting into serious trouble. In the next chapter I want to tell you how I won a gold medal in the special athletics events held for deaf schoolchildren.

9. Gold for God

I've always enjoyed sports and athletics, and have a large pile of certificates to prove it. I'm very proud of one of them, for high jump, which was presented to me by Steve Ovett himself when he came to our sports day when I was younger, at boarding school.

When I joined the large secondary school at Tonbridge, the sports facilities were much better and there was more competition, which was good for me. I entered this side of school life with enthusiasm and was delighted when I won my athletics colours. The biggest events for me were when I was entered in the PHD's team for the Southern Deaf Sports Association. These were held at the Crystal Palace.

On the first occasion when I was fourteen I was entered for the hundred metres, the two hundred metres and the high jump. It was a good day out. We went there by car. Each teacher took some pupils and some of the parents took their children. My mother drove me up to Crystal Palace. I did not eat very much in case I got a stomach upset.

It was exciting to be running at such an important stadium. The track is very good, made of rubber so that runners do not damage their feet (or their knees if they fall!). Everything looked so big and of course the spectator stand was not as full as it would be for an international event. I did not do too well in the hundred metres but the two hundred metres was an exciting race. I ran faster and faster and finished first in the heats. In the final race I finished third. I also finished third in the high jump, so I was very happy. I felt awful after running, too weak ever to want to run again. I needed a rest, and then I was all right.

The following year I wanted to try throwing the discus. I practised and practised with a teacher. At first I found it very hard. He showed me how to turn around and around to throw it. I kept on trying and gradually improved. To begin with my shots only went about fifteen metres. I had read that the winner's shot in the previous year had been much further. I tried again and again and at last I reached seventeen metres. That was enough progress for the first day, so I went back to work in the classroom. After a few weeks I reached eighteen metres. My teacher said I was good enough to enter for the Crystal Palace sports for the deaf again. On this occasion our team was much smaller and weaker. I was entered for the two hundred metres, the high jump and the discus. When we arrived, I began the day with the two hundred metre heats. I had a good start and finished first. I clocked about twenty-four seconds. That was the fastest I'd ever run the two hundred metres in my life. I had always won the running races at my previous school ever since I was eight. When I was thirteen I had clocked 15.5 seconds for a hundred metres, just about 1.2 seconds behind the school record for my age. I was sorry that I'd never made that record. Now I shall never be that age again to try. But my favourite length of race is really the two hundred metres, which I enjoy very much.

The next event for me was the high jump. To begin with it was very low and I jumped over easily. I saw a tall boy knock the cane off three times. He was the one I'd decided in my mind would win it, so I felt a bit more hopeful. I carried on successfully until the line reached my neck, at about 1.28 metres. I finished second and was delighted.

Then I went over to the discus nets where I met another competitor, John Tyrrell. I was to meet him a year or so later when I went on to college. His school team were all shouting out, 'The greatest boy for us! The greatest boy for us!' to support him. 'Oh,' I thought, 'I shall make sure I'm the greatest!' My first throw went nineteen metres. I was amazed. After my first throw I was in third place. I put everything I'd got into the second throw. It went beyond twenty metres and was the furthest throw so far. I was now in the lead. My last two throws were not very good, but no one else had been able to beat me, so I was very happy.

Two of the other competitors who had come in our team, Philip and Rachel, had also finished first in their sports. 'Perhaps we'll be chosen to go to Birmingham for the finals?' we said to each other.

At last it was time for the two hundred metre final. I only finished third and clocked about twenty-five seconds. I was running at full speed and was just a few metres from the finishing line when I felt a boy behind me trying to overtake. I was nearly at the finishing line and could feel the draught of the boy passing me. I put on an extra spurt. I came third and he came fourth, about .001 of a second behind me. Oh! That was a near one. Phew! I only just managed it.

I was tired by now, but we still had the relay race to run. We finished about fifth or sixth. We returned home exhausted, but very pleased with ourselves.

Shortly afterwards, as we'd hoped, Rachel, Philip and I were chosen to represent the South of England at the finals held in Birmingham. If you win at Birmingham and do very well there, you may be chosen for the world finals, held in West Germany. Would any of us make that, we wondered?

A teacher took us by train to Birmingham. I enjoyed the experience of crossing London by Underground. When we passed through Goodge Street station, where there had been a fire a few days before, I smelled the air, like burning bacon. We left London from Euston station, the first time I'd been there. We had a good journey on the Inter-City and when we arrived at Birmingham a teacher from a local deaf school met us. He knew one of our teachers and he'd invited us all to lunch. We ate it at the same table as the staff. I don't know why there wasn't room for us to eat with the other pupils.

After lunch we were taken to the stadium. Philip and I had a practice run round the track, which was the same type as at Crystal Palace. The stands were much smaller, and were full of people. I wondered why the finals were held at Birmingham. Far more people could have come to the Crystal Palace.

The weather was not too bad and to begin with I watched Philip and Rachel race. Then I went to the discus nets and talked to some of the other competitors and their friends. Some of them told me who was the strongest and whom they thought would win. We were allowed three throws. A tall, thin boy whom I was later to meet at college was throwing very well. He won the competition that day with an amazing throw of between twenty-nine and thirty metres. I finished fourth with a throw of twenty-four metres which was good for me. Philip meanwhile had won a gold medal in his relay. Rachel came third in her eight hundred metre race, and won a bronze medal. So Hugh Christie School did very well and our teachers were pleased with us. When the games ended it was announced that the South East had won, and we went out in the stadium. We had beaten teams from the rest of England, Wales and Northern Ireland. We were all very tired on the way home.

In the morning at school, Mr Harding took a photograph of us for the local newspaper with details of how we'd done. All this time I was dreaming about the next year's finals at Birmingham where I was determined to win the discus throwing. Could it be possible, Lord? Perhaps. Little did I know that something was going to happen which nearly prevented my going to the Birmingham Finals at all, but which made my going and the results I got there even more remarkable. People were amazed at what happened and I will tell you about it.

During the winter season at school when I was in my fifth year we played a variety of games such as volley ball, handball, table tennis, gymnastics and indoor hockey. I enjoyed gymnastics best, especially leaping over the horse from the spring board. I was happy at school during this period and working well. Until December, when everything altered for me. During a PE lesson we were all doing gymnastics, jumping over the horse and having fun. Sometimes we were just fooling about. Some of us jumped over the horse without touching it. We landed on a big, soft mat. My last jump over was the best, a good clear jump. The teacher asked all of us if we wanted the horse away so that we could practise jumping and rolling on the mat. This was something we enjoyed so we put the horse away.

I went first. I ran to the soft springs which pushed me up. I put both my feet on to them, then jumped up and rolled over. Suddenly I saw the wall coming too close to me just as I was coming down. I don't remember how many times I rolled. I thought that I must stop or I would hit the wall. It was far too close. I did an emergency stop; my body hurtled down. As I landed, my right cheek bone hit my knee. It was just as if I had braked hard in a car without a seat belt. My cheek bone thudded into my knee. Next I fell backwards. As I did so, I realised I'd done something to my face. I was nowhere near the wall now. I got up quickly and put my hand on to the right side of my face.

The teacher saw me. 'What have you done?' he asked, but I just rushed out of the hall to the changing room. I kept walking up and down, holding my painful cheek and wondering what I'd done. The teacher hurried in to see me. He said, 'What happened? I saw you go over with a bang.' He looked at my face. 'My, you've got a black eye to end all black eyes!' he said, and we both laughed, because we did not realise that it was any worse than that. My face looked horrible, as if a bone had fallen out of it. I felt very cold and the teacher told me to go into his office to keep warm. I sat there feeling quite awful. As soon as the teacher had told the rest of the class what to do he came back to me and told me to change back into my clothes, and go to see the head of the PHD, Mr Harding.

He was very busy when I went in, but he suddenly looked up and saw my face. What a shock he got. He made me sit down and said that we must ring for my mother to collect me. He told me to watch his finger. He moved it to the left side of my eyes and they were able to follow it. What a relief, my eyes were all right. He then moved his finger to my right side. I found that I could move my eyes up but not to the right or down. I was feeling very ill by now. I could not speak well and at one point had to rush off to be sick. At last my mother came with my little brother Colin. She had a talk with Mr Harding and I went home in the car. None of us realised that I had broken a bone. On the way out of school I waved from the back seat to several friends who had been in the gym with me.

When I got home I went up to bed and was sick again. This hurt my cheek bone very much. In the evening my father and other brother Greg came home and had a look at me. The next day I was not fit to go to school and my face looked awful. I went with my mother down to the green-grocer's where I worked on Saturdays. We told him that I would not be fit to work there until after Christmas. That evening, my father looked at my face again and decided that I should go to see the doctor. At the surgery, the doctor took one look at me and said that I must go to Pembury Hospital immediately for an X-ray.

After the X-rays, the doctor looked at the pictures and told us that my cheek bone was damaged. I was amazed that I had not realised this before. He told us to go to a special hospital, the Queen Victoria Hospital in East Grinstead that afternoon. So I took the X-rays with us. I told my mother that I wanted my father to come with me. She rang him at work and he said he would be able to arrange to have the afternoon off.

So we set off, a very pleasant drive through the Sussex countryside. At the hospital we had the usual wait before we were seen. Finally I went into the doctor's room. He was wearing green clothes and a hat to stop his hair falling into anything. He looked at my face. He put his fingers on my face and inside my mouth to check it. He touched his finger on my right cheek and asked me whether I could feel it. I said, 'No'. So he touched the other cheek and I said, 'Yes'. Next he moved his finger about to test my eyes just as Mr Harding had done. Then he had long talks with my father, and we went for further photos and X-rays. The light was very bright. I could not see anything because the background was too dark for my eyes. My father explained to me that I would have to have an operation on Friday but that meanwhile we could go home. The next evening I went out to play chess with some friends. I wore my sunglasses to conceal the full horror of my face. I went into the room where my friends were playing.

Someone looked up and said, 'Hello Phillip,' and went on playing his game. The next moment I swished off my glasses. Everyone was amazed at the transformation. They crowded round me asking what I'd done, and what was the matter. My father who was still there told them about my accident. When he'd left I settled down to play chess for the evening. Sometimes my friends made jokes about my appearance and when I laughed it hurt so much I had to tell them to stop cracking jokes. 'Sorry,' they said, and smiled.

The next morning I had no tea or breakfast because of my operation. My father took me to the hospital. I was very worried about what was going to happen to me, but he explained what he could and told me not to worry. I know that my family and friends were praying for me at this time. It was soon time for him to drive back to work. I undressed and put on the long white gown which everyone has to wear for an operation. Then I got my Dad's old dressing gown out of my case and put that on. Before he went I'd joked with him that the moths might fly out of it because it was more than twenty years old. Then I sat on the bed feeling hungry and lonely. I was not allowed anything to eat before the operation. After what seemed like ages a doctor came to me and he wrote down on a piece of paper that my operation would begin at about twelve-thirty, and that a nurse would give me some medicine first. Then he checked my blood pressure and chatted to me about the operation and left. I was in a great deal of pain all this time and was not thinking very clearly. I cannot remember that I prayed at all. I was just thinking of the pain. A nurse came and told me to take off my dressing gown and get into bed. When I had done this, I was injected in the customary place, my behind.

'What is it?' I wanted to know.

'It is to help you to go to sleep for the operation,' the nurse told me.

I waited for about half an hour, not feeling at all sleepy. Then I saw the trolley arrive by my bedside. The nurse helped me to get on. I lay down and was pushed through the corridors and, for some of the way, into the freezing world outside. Finally we went into the operation room. It looked very green with some lights above me. I remembered that the doctor said that the operation would take about half an hour to do. Next someone tried to give me another injection in my arm, but I swung it out of the way and asked what it was in case it was a drug which I didn't want to use. The anaesthetist could not understand me so a nurse came to talk to me.

'It's only to help you to go to sleep quickly,' she said. The anaesthetic worked quickly. I thought I was dead. I did not dream at all. When I woke up I saw everything white, very white. Oh, what a beautiful whiteness it was. I was in heaven. I saw myself all white. I did not see anyone else, except Jesus. His clothing was all white too.

It was an extraordinary experience. Sometime later I wrote a song about this.

> *Did I Walk into the White?*
> Did I walk into the white?
> I went for an operation
> Suddenly I felt dead and
> No dreaming at all.
> When I woke up, I saw
> Everything white, very white.
> Oh! What a beautiful colour,
> I was in heaven.
> I saw myself all white.
> I saw no one else there
> But I saw Jesus, shining white too.

Praise the Lord O my soul.
I thought that's the way to heaven.
My eyes opened a crack
And could not see very well.
But someone gave me
A drink of cold water.
It was a fresh one.
I felt myself. No, I wasn't dead
But I knew that I was not in heaven.
Oh, dear, I knew, and went back to sleep.
Jesus, I love you . . .

After a sleep I awoke to find myself back in bed. It was about seven thirty in the evening. A nurse asked me if I wanted a cup of tea. I said slowly, 'Yes, please,' but she did not understand my blurred speech. I nodded my head for yes. Then I got out of bed and was sick in the toilet. A man came along and was angry with me for making a mess in the toilet. He showed me a little basin and told me that next time I was to be sick in that. Too late now! Because I was deaf he did not understand me or make himself very clear.

That night I could not get to sleep for a long time, but finally I drifted off. When I woke at about one in the morning I saw a piece of paper on my desk. It must have been there for several hours. I leaned across and picked it up to read. It said, 'Your father phoned tonight and says, "How are you?" We told him you were all right but too sleepy to talk to him.' I was pleased to find that message and went off to sleep again. Suddenly it was six o'clock in the morning. Nurses switched the lights on and came round giving medicine to us all. What a waste of sleep. How awful to be woken up at that hour.

Soon I was ready to sit up and have some breakfast. Later I was allowed to dress and went to the X-ray department for a final check that the operation had been successful. I was surprised how weak and wobbly I felt. Also my back was beginning to hurt a little. I walked like an old man and could not straighten my back. I had some lunch, but could not eat much. Sometimes I went out to the toilets to look at my face in the mirror. I could see some black hairs sticking out. I didn't know what it was. 'I must have a shave soon,' I thought. But it was a stitch put in by the surgeon. Just one.

Late in the afternoon my parents visited me and we stayed talking for about an hour. At last the doctors came on their rounds and told us that everything had gone well and that I could go home. By the time we'd got to Tunbridge Wells my back had got much worse. I tried to lie down but could not. The pain was so bad. I held on to my mother's hand and tried to lower myself into the bed. Something was very wrong with my back and it took several months after the operation to get better.

I was not allowed back to school until the last day of term before the Christmas holidays came, when I went in to see everyone. I saw my PE teacher and told him that I was not to do PE for three months according to the hospital. 'Farewell to winning the discus throw at Birmingham!' I thought to myself. With no PE and athletics for so long I would never be in training in time to be selected for the school team. I said, 'Happy Christmas,' to all my friends and teachers. My face was not black and bruised as when they'd last seen me, but my eye was bloodshot. It took two or three months to clear.

It was back to school the next term, after Christmas, but with no PE or games. I made sure not to get into any fights or rough games. I didn't want to damage my cheekbone again. I was longing to join in sports as soon as I could. But there were the summer exams to work for and I'd missed a lot of lessons the previous term.

At last I was back to full strength, and was able to take up sports again. I used to run round the school for a while to get myself into training. I also used to play volley ball. In the summer term I decided that my exams must take first place, so I studied hard and tried to forget about sports.

Then – farewell to the CSE exams. I felt that I had not done too badly. Now I could give my full time to training for the Crystal Palace sports again. I took up weightlifting to strengthen me and found this better than running as I'd got so much heavier. Once again I was chosen to go to Crystal Palace. I was glad about that small excitement, because I knew I had little hope of going up to Birmingham. We travelled up by car and on the way I was worrying about my performance. I'd had so little sport in the last year that I did not think that I would do very well. Perhaps I should quit altogether. But I thought I should wait and see if God told me to quit.

It was a blazing hot day, and I got sunburn on my shoulders. I was wearing the Hugh Christie school sports vest and white shorts. I came third in the high jump. Not too bad. I saw that Philip had won his eight hundred metre race. I went over to the discus nets, only to find that I was the only person there. Everyone else had finished throwing while I was in the high jump. I asked the teacher if I could see how far the furthest throw had gone, but she refused. If I had been there with the others I would have been able to get my eye in. I decided to try as hard as I could. I threw three of my best throws. I finished second. I was amazed to hear that the winner's throw was two or three metres further than mine. I knew then that I would not go to Birmingham for the finals.

I heard that Rachel had won the shot-put. Both she and Philip came up to me and said that if I could only win the two hundred metre race, I could go to Birmingham even now. I told them that I would try but I knew that I was not up to running my fastest ever, as the accident had slowed me down. Philip said he would give me his best shoes to help me run faster. I saw they were very good ones he'd borrowed from school. I ran to the start of the two hundred metre line. The flag went down and I ran off quickly. But I did not have the staying power. I got very tired and finished fifth. Philip and Rachel were sorry for me that I was not going to Birmingham.

In spite of my injuries I'd not done too badly that day. We all returned happily home. Soon I received some good

news. The boy who had won the discus event did not want
to go up to Birmingham, for some reason. I was asked to
take his place! Once again we three heroes could compete
together.

Particularly on this occasion, I prayed to God to help me
at Birmingham. I knew that even now I was not fully fit. Mr
Sharpe took Philip and me by train. Rachel went by car
with her parents. We enjoyed going out with Mr Sharpe
because he always got in a muddle on journeys, and found
it hard to organise. This journey was no exception. Instead
of the speedy, efficient Inter-City train, Mr Sharpe somehow managed to choose a slow, stopping train, via North-
ampton. We were so bored we whiled away the time
playing cards. Even Mr Sharpe joined in.

It was typical Birmingham weather when we arrived: wet
and dismal. We caught a taxi to the stadium and met up
with Rachel. We changed and got ready for our events. I
had to wait a long time for the discus event and felt quite
cold and miserable. Gradually many people arrived and the
spectator stands filled up. I was able to watch Rachel come
third in the shot-put and Philip come either third or fourth
in the eight hundred metres. At last it was time for my
event. Rachel and Philip urged me to do my best to win the
gold medal for the school.

'Perhaps. I will try,' I told them.

I left them and went out on to the field and limbered up
and got myself ready. We were allowed a warm-up throw
which I thought was a good idea. I could see that some of
the other competitors were bigger than me. We all talked to
each other, trying to work out who would win. We all
thought it would be the tallest person there. My first throw
was not my strongest and it landed about twenty-seven
metres away. At my second throw, God helped me. I felt
I'd thrown it weakly again, but God lifted it and carried it
far away to twenty-eight metres, my record so far. Thank
you Lord for blowing the wind for my discus. At this point
my throw put me into the lead. We still had the third and
fourth throws to come. Perhaps the bigger competitors

would reserve all their strength for them. There was nothing special about my attempts when my turn came. I did not do very well at all. But my second shot had beaten all the others. I had won the discus event for our school for the first time in Birmingham. I'd won the gold medal and become the number one under-seventeen deaf discus thrower in Britain for one year. I ended David Buxton's reign. I met him later at college and found out that he too was a Christian.

I went up to receive my award. I was very happy. I was thankful and full of praise. My heart was full of love, from the Lord. A man gave me my gold medal and Mr Sharpe took several photographs of us for the local newspaper.

We were all worn out by this time. Rachel sailed off in the car, and Mr Sharpe made sure of an Inter-City for a fast journey back to London. When my father met me at Tonbridge he was delighted to hear my news.

An amusing incident happened a week later. As all my exams at school were over there was no reason for me to go to school. Of course I was longing to share my excitement with all my friends. About a week later, I got up early and went on the usual bus to school. Quite naturally, nobody took any special notice of me. I was just one schoolboy amongst many. However, as the bus neared Tonbridge and more people got on many of them stared at me. I did not know why. I felt very embarrassed and looked out of the window for a long time. But each time we stopped at a bus stop, more people kept staring at me. I didn't know where to put myself. I tried hard to make myself look back naturally at them. I thought perhaps they thought I was a spy, or a murderer or something. But when I got to school I understood everything.

Someone had got hold of a copy of the local Tonbridge paper. Philip, Rachel and I were on the front page. We all had a laugh about my embarrassing journey. On the way home I did not want the same thing to happen to me, so I read a newspaper to hide my face. I didn't want anyone to stop me or to ask me to sign a book. Several years later I

wrote a song about my accident. It puzzled me why it had
happened, though through it I experienced God helping
me.

10. Falling in Love

A lot happened to me during the autumn of 1979 when I was almost fifteen. Not only was I baptised at church, I also fell in love with Anne, a beautiful girl at school. I did not know her name to begin with, but saw her in classes over in the main school. She was not a pupil in the PHD. One day I looked her full in the face and opened my eyes wildly at her. All through the next lesson I thought about her. She sat behind me to the right where she could watch me. I found it difficult to turn round to look at her. Were we thinking of falling in love I wondered? The first problem I wanted to sort out was whether she was a Christian. I could not ask her as my speech was not clear enough.

During lunch time I saw her leave school to go home. She saw me, but could not stop to talk as she had to hurry to be back in time for afternoon lessons. I stood there wondering whether she would become my very first hearing girl friend. I found it hard to pluck up courage to speak to her as she did not make the first move to speak to me. I felt very nervous because she was a girl and a hearing girl, not deaf like me. What would she think of my speech? It was easy enough to speak to the other deaf pupils in the PHD, but this was different. But never mind. It didn't matter. It was life and the time of life to mix with the hearing.

One day when everyone was pouring out of school to go home I walked thoughtfully down the drive. I stopped and waited for Anne to catch me up and asked her if I could walk along the road with her. I talked to her and tried to say what I wanted, but I was overcome with my feelings and was quite tongue-tied. I dared not ask her what she thought about me. If only I could speak properly. She went very shy and red-faced but she kept smiling at me. I enjoyed talking to her, but did she understand me? My heart beat very fast.

One day I heard that her father was coming to the school to discuss careers for Anne. I waited around the car park and saw him arrive. One thing puzzled me. Anne was fifteen and I imagined that her father would be about thirty-five to forty-five. When I saw him he looked much older, at least fifty-five. What had made him age so much? From my human biology books I tried to find out what caused a face to age prematurely. Drugs seemed to be the answer. But surely Anne's father could not be on illegal drugs? There must be some other cause.

Anne was thin and beautiful. Whenever I could I talked to her. Because my love was so strong I never brought myself to ask her where she lived. But I did not spend all my spare time at school talking to her. I knew there was a risk of not doing well in exams if I spent too much time with her. Each time I ended a conversation with her and said, 'Goodbye,' my heart beat much faster as I walked off.

I realised more and more that if I wanted to become her boy friend I must find out whether she was a Christian or not. I knew that if she were not a Christian then no way could I be her boy friend.

During the lunch hour one day I tried to follow Anne home to see where she lived. I did it secretly, I didn't want her to see me. I walked far behind and kept watching in case she turned her head round and saw me. I had to be alert to move quickly. If I saw she was about to cross a road and look in my direction I hid in a front garden or drive. I don't know what anyone who saw me must have thought. I might even have got bitten by a dog if I'd rushed in a gate with a warning about a dog.

I followed Anne in this way on numerous occasions, hiding and dodging. Sometimes I followed her just for a short way. Gradually as I began to know the route I followed her further and further. On one occasion I had followed Anne almost to her home. Just as she turned and

saw me clearly for the first time, her brother happened to
come up behind me, on his way home. He called out to her
to wait for him to catch her up and I quickly walked off
down another road. I thought to myself, 'waste'. Later I
tried to see where they'd gone and could not see them
anywhere. I gave up and went back to school.

Again and again I tracked Anne home and at last I
managed to get as far as her house. After many turnings
and crossing many roads I made it. She lived on a council
estate. The front doors looked out over a footpath and the
proper road ran behind the houses. At last I'd found out
where she lived. But I was too nervous to knock on the
door. I had a silly idea that I'd need a police pass to get in,
because I was an unknown person to Anne's family. I knew
she had a sister but I had not yet seen her.

Several months later I decided to give Anne up. It was
difficult to get to know her and I was not sure that it was
right. To my surprise, my teacher who also taught Anne's
brother said to me one day, 'Did you know that Anne is
moving soon?' I did not know that she knew I was even
interested in Anne. 'Kevin her brother told me they are
moving out of their council house to a house of their own at
the other end of town.'

I was so surprised that she should talk to me about Anne,
that all I answered was 'What? Thank you very much!' I
never went and found out exactly where it was, because I'd
decided to end the friendship. Perhaps after all her dad had
aged with worry about his mortgage!

I returned to my school studies with more concentration.
I was looking forward to leaving school but I felt sure that I
would never find a job. I went to see my careers officer and
she told me about various jobs. I had no idea there were so
many openings. She also gave me a booklet about a deaf
college. It was outside London, but I did not like the idea of
going there in case I got into trouble as I had at boarding
school, but I thought about it and wrote off to ask for an
interview.

My parents took me and then went off for the day. I had

various tests to do before I could be accepted. The English exam was hopeless. I just could not do it at all. The next exam was technical drawing. This was taken by a very helpful middle-aged teacher. He told me when to start and stop. There were hundreds of questions. Some of them had to be done very fast, twenty-five in five minutes. I finished ninety questions and got them all right. The maths was not so good. I was too slow. After these tests I went to lunch with the other students in the college.

Later my parents arrived and we talked with the staff. It was a small college and only offered limited subjects. A wider curriculum was studied at a larger nearby college. The head teacher said that I had been accepted to start the following September.

I was still not sure whether I wanted to go. Wouldn't it be better to leave school now and try to get a job? I was not sure. I kept thinking about it, but could not make up my mind. Perhaps I did not want to bother with more school work. Mum was keen for me to go and she invited one of her Christian friends round. In front of her Mum asked me whether I'd made my mind up or not. I told her that I thought I wouldn't go to college. The friend had a good talk with me. She was very fond of me and wanted the best for me. She reminded me that love is not selfish and that perhaps it would be helpful not only to me but to my family too if I went on to further education. I could see what she meant and she went on to explain that college would be a new life, quite different from school. It would be boarding again, but with only about twenty students and four teachers. Her enthusiasm and good advice helped me to decide. By the time she was ready to leave, I told them I would go to college.

During the summer holidays I waited eagerly for my CSE results and was delighted when they came. I'd gained a grade 2 in every subject except human biology where I'd gained a grade 1.

What about Anne all this time? I'd seen her around at school of course, but love had not blossomed. I left school, went to college and finally went out to work. It was when I was almost eighteen that I thought about her again and decided I would like to see her once more. To begin with I had no idea how I could manage it. I'd once written a song about her and had written at the bottom, 'I'll never see her again. I will never see her again.' But you cannot organise your feelings so easily. My mind was changed and I did all I could to find her in the local telephone directory. I was not sure of her address. If only I'd listened more carefully when my teacher had told me. However I could make a reason-able guess as to which name in the directory might be hers. I made a list of several names and numbers.

The next day I went to see my good friend Tim who worked with me and who also went to the same church. I told him about my problem and asked him whether he would ring these various numbers for me. Tim was not so sure. He felt very embarrassed about ringing up strange people and asking them whether they had a daughter called Anne. Let alone then going on to say that he was speaking on behalf of Phillip who would like to marry her. No, it was just not on. 'I can't do it,' he said. 'It's a crazy idea.'

I touched his arm, and said, 'Stop being so silly. Just ring up and say you are ringing on behalf of a deaf friend, and can they help you?'

Finally he agreed. I gave him the first number to ring. I watched his face eagerly the whole time. The first number was no good. Tim dialled the second number. I saw him speaking excitedly. Only the second number and we'd got the right one. Tim spoke to Anne's brother. I saw him laughing. He put the receiver down and said, 'I've got their new address. They've moved again.'

'Thank you very much,' I said to Tim. 'If I write out a list of questions will you ring again another day and get the answers for me?' Tim found all this very difficult. He was a good friend and wanted to help me. He knew that I could not use the phone. But what difficult things I was asking him to do! About a week later I gave him the questions. I wanted to make sure that Anne would be happy to see me

again. He was to tell her that I wanted to come to see her
and that we would ring again when she'd had time to think
about it.

. Tantalisingly Tim said that he would ring her up 'some
time' and 'one evening'. That of course was far too slow for
me, but I had to be patient.

He did in fact ring that night but there was no one in. The
next evening he was successful and Anne herself answered
the phone. When Tim said he was ringing on my behalf she
sounded a bit shocked and surprised, but still friendly. 'It
was a long time ago that we were at school together,' she
said.

Tim did not give me all the details of this phone call but
gave me the answers to my questions. Anne wanted to
know what I wanted to see her about. I must ring back and
tell her, then she would decide if she wanted to meet me
again.

I was amazed that she gave such a sensible answer. Tim
told me some more news about her which I drank in
eagerly. Apparently Anne was working in Mothercare and
had actually seen me walking about town. Tim told her
where I was working and she asked him whether he knew a
friend of hers who was also working there. Tim said he did
not know her, even though she'd been there for about ten
months. But it was a huge building with so many people
working there, that it was not possible to know everyone.
Finally Tim told me that Anne worked on Saturdays but
was off on Tuesdays.

What a lot to think about. I thanked Tim very much. I
was so grateful to him. Not that phoning via a friend is the
best way to carry on a romance. I now had to work out a
harder list of questions, to help Anne to decide whether she
would see me or not. The list I gave long suffering Tim next
read as follows:

How long have you been working at Mothercare?
What was your first job?

I thought you wanted to go into dance and drama – what happened to that?

I want to show you a book which I am writing, but I cannot tell you the name of it because it is a secret. It may come as a surprise to you.

I have no ideas when I shall see you. Are you out in the evenings? I know you work Saturdays, but I work on Tuesdays.

Do you look different now?

As you can imagine I could not wait to get the answers to all these questions. I went round to Tim several times but he'd been unable to get any answer. I had to wait yet another day for him to ring. The next night I went round again and he said he'd forgotten. How could he? It was never out of my thoughts. Finally on Friday I went round again and he said he'd rung her. He gave me the list of answers. I grabbed it eagerly from his hand and read them. This is what the message said:

I rang Anne. She's been working for two years, firstly in a solicitor's, then at Mothercare. She would have liked to have done dance and drama, but she thinks she missed the chance. She does some now in the evenings. She goes to some society for that. It was a very nice phone call. She says she's different now, she's changed her hair style. She looks older but she still has the same face. She says she will see you to look at your book or whatever you want to show her, but it's difficult to find time. She could manage a lunch time. She doesn't know when her lunch time is until she gets into work each day. She has only one hour for lunch and she is out every evening, working on Saturday and busy on her day off. She will try and sort out a time.

Tim said he had talked on the phone for about five minutes. I asked him what kind of job Anne did in Mothercare. 'Perhaps selling prams?' I laughed. I wanted to sit

down and have a long discussion all about the phone call
and about Anne with Tim, but he had something else on his
mind which he wanted to talk about. I did my best to
concentrate. He wanted me to help in an amusing fancy
dress treasure hunt the next day. He wanted me to dress up
as a tramp and wait by the cinema for the youth group to
arrive to hand them the next clue. Tim had seen me dressed
up as a tramp before at various parties and thought I looked
good.

I agreed to the plan. Tim himself was dressing up as a
gangster and another friend Mark was dressing up as some
other character. Tim went on enthusiastically telling me all
the details about where we had to meet the next day. 'It's
up to you how you dress, but don't get arrested by the
police,' he said. All the time he was talking about the
treasure hunt, I was thinking about Anne.

As soon as he stopped I said, 'Tim, did you give Anne
your phone number?'

'No, I didn't,' Tim said.

'You must next time,' I said. 'But it's too late now.
Anyway we haven't lost touch with her.'

The next day I tried to write a note to Anne, including
our telephone number. In the afternoon I got all my old
clothes ready to dress up as the tramp in the evening. I also
got some make-up, a newspaper, my pocket Bible and a
hat. I found some old boots. They were dirty and messy. I
put them in a plastic bag, and everything in a large holdall.
At about two thirty in the afternoon I went down into town.
My holdall was heavy and the streets were crowded with
shoppers. First of all I went to find my brother Greg who
was working at a Saturday job with W.H. Smith. I went in
and had a chat to him. Then I went off to find Anne. The
shop where she worked was close by. I waited outside
Mothercare to try to see her through the window. There
were so many racks of clothes and prams that I could not
see easily into the shop. I realised it would be impossible to
see her like that. So I went inside and looked around. My
heart was beating faster and faster. I waited for one of the

assistants to finish speaking to a customer then I went up to her. I put my bag down and put my hand in my pocket. I got out the note with Anne's name on it. I showed it to her. She said, 'Yes, I know her. Do you want to see her?'

'Yes please!' I said. My heart beat much faster, but I could not stop it. They were heavy beats. Suddenly I saw the assistant give the note to a girl who must be Anne. I could not believe it was her. She looked so different from schooldays. She saw me and looked at the note and came round to me. I told her that Tim had forgotten to give her my phone number and I thought it would be helpful for her to have it. She understood what I was saying.

I was amazed at how well she did understand because the last time I'd spoken to her at school she'd only laughed. This time everything went well. My only reaction to her now was a longing to get better at speaking to her. Having handed over my note I hurried out of the shop and made my way to meet my friends as planned. Gradually my heart beat slowed down!

On the way I met Rachel, a girl from our youth group. She told me that Tim was at home playing his guitar. I arrived at his house, rang the bell and opened the door and went inside. I put my bag down and waited, but no one came. Of course I could not hear him playing his guitar and he could not hear me because of the guitar. I did not know which room to look in. I thought I'd try upstairs, so I went up and found him. He stopped playing and I told him all about my visit to Mothercare and my conversation with Anne. He was very pleased for me.

Later when the other young people arrived I did not let them see me, as it was to be a surprise that I was to be there dressed up as a tramp. I hid upstairs and had to wait for a long time in the bedroom. I sat on a chair thinking of nothing. There were no feelings within Anne, I was sure. Perhaps I would get hurt through loving her. She was very beautiful. I'd seen that. I thought of love music, happy and sad. If only I could express it, but it would be hard to put my feelings into music.

At last Tim came up and told me that all the others had
gone and it was time to get dressed. I asked him who was in
each of the three groups and he explained everything to
me. Just as I got dressed, Jenny, a latecomer, arrived and
saw me. We could not let her go and join the others now, so
she had to dress up too. Meanwhile I was putting make-up
on my face. Not Mum's make-up, but black and brown
polish. I smudged it over my face to make me look weather-
beaten and dirty. I also put red lipstick round my eyes to
make me look very tired and drunk. Finally I put on my old
warm coat and hat. I carried a wine bottle full of water
stuffed into a paper bag. I staggered down the stairs like a
drunken man but no one saw me. Outside the front door I
put on my boots. It was very cold and dark.

We all drove down into town in Mark's car. Mark's car
was really old but it worked well. In was a 1971 Austin
Morris 1300 GT. When we arrived at the back of Boots we
got out and walked along the narrow lane which led to the
main road. Tim saw someone behind us and shouted to us
to start running away to our places. Someone gave me a
push and I ran and ran in my heavy boots. We thought it
must be some of the youth group following us. We did not
want them to see us. Mark took his hat off to run faster. I
speeded up getting very hot in all my tramp clothes. Jenny
ran with me. At last we reached the cinema where we were
to play our part. We found some seats by the telephone
kiosks and sat down. I pretended to be asleep, or just
dozing, sitting upright, and Jenny sat beside me. We sat
and waited and waited for some of the youth group to
arrive. Meanwhile I offered Jenny a drink from my bottle
of wine which she accepted. I had a drink too. Because of
all the clothes we had on and the fact that we'd hurried
through the town, we were both warm.

Two or three times, Jenny went to see if anyone was
coming, but no one was in sight. Jenny decided to go off to
find Tim near Boots and see what was happening. She soon
returned and said she could not find him. I told her that as
he was a gangster, he might be hiding behind Boots, so off

she went again and did not return. I went on waiting, wondering what people were thinking of me sitting there. I had my hat pulled down over my nose so that no one would recognise me. They would just think I was a tramp. I tucked the bottle under my arm and swung it slowly about and then fell asleep. At about eight o'clock the first group came. They ran to the cinema steps and looked around them. I pulled my hat down lower still and went on sleeping. Suddenly someone jumped on to the seat and I woke up a bit and fell asleep again, still acting my part. Philip, one of the group shook me to get up. I woke up and saw him. I made noises like a drunk man. Philip laughed. I got up and met the first group of young people talking in a funny way. I breathed down my nose and up into my mouth and asked them what they wanted. They all laughed and I gave them the next card for the treasure hunt. I asked them if anyone wanted to buy anything and pulled out an old oily pair of pants. Kay didn't like the idea at all and I put them away. So off they went and I sat down to wait for the second group to arrive. When they came to the cinema I waited quietly pretending to be asleep for quite a while. No one came over to me. I slept on. Suddenly someone touched me. I did the same as with the first group and gave them their card wrapped in the oily pants. I told them how far ahead the other group was and they thought they would soon catch them up. There was only one more group to come. I was enjoying myself.

Suddenly I leapt out of my seat, rushed across the road just as the lights went green. I had to run quickly because I could see cars coming through the lights. I rushed to the Town Hall steps. I'd seen a young boy from our youth group coming along on his bike. This was cheating, because no bikes were allowed. He was from the third group and was watching where the others went to report back to the rest of his group, so that they could save time.

Quickly I got out my newspaper and made a bed with it, and went to sleep on the Town Hall steps. I did not see someone creep up to me and take my hat off, because my eyes were closed. Suddenly I got up and pretended to be frightened of them. I gave them the last card. When they had gone off I drank all the water in my bottle, threw it in the litter bin and waited for Mark to come. He soon arrived and took me back in the car to Tim's house. When I went into the lounge everyone clapped. They had enjoyed my performance and thought I'd been the best. I washed and dressed and joined them downstairs for games and a hot drink. Tim said he'd been pleased too with my tramp acting. I wonder what Anne would have thought if she had seen me?

During the next few weeks both Anne and I were very busy, too busy to be able to see each other. I went into Mothercare on several occasions to ask for her but she was always at lunch or out. I kept going back but never found her again. Once I saw her walking past me in the street but I didn't realise it was her until she had gone. Much later I saw her again, but did not try to stop her to speak to. So really my friendship never developed with Anne. Partly it was because I did not have much confidence, because I was deaf. Partly she was not a Christian and I knew that I should only get involved with a girl who loved Jesus like me.

Now I knew that I meant the words of my song:

I will never understand her.
I will never see her again. I will never see her again.

11. Trouble at Margate

The light hearted evening when I dressed up as a tramp gives a good picture of the relaxed and happy atmosphere in the youth group and the way I was accepted as one of them. But this took time to achieve. It did not happen quickly and together we went through some difficult patches. The young people were a friendly bunch, but like any group of teenagers occasionally thoughtless. Looking back now, I can see obvious reasons why things went wrong. When we went out together, we seldom managed to take a note pad and pencil. This meant that no one could jot down important information for me. If we were travelling in the mini-bus, most of the conversation was flung over people's shoulders, or tossed rapidly backwards and forwards. In this situation I was at a disadvantage. I could not lip read. I could not even see everyone's face. Being teenagers too many a conversation ended in muffled giggles. I often thought they were laughing about me or talking about me. I felt very upset and lonely. I realise now that they did not mean to leave me out of their gossip or mean to make me feel an outsider. They were just being themselves. In a lively group it was bound to happen.

When we all went out together everyone was excited and only the few bothered to face me and speak clearly to me and wait patiently for my answer. At that time as I was still fairly new there, not many members of the group could actually understand my speech. All of this was a recipe for disaster. For example I would give someone in the youth group a message and he would think he'd understood me. He had in fact misunderstood me and got the message

wrong. In all good faith he'd repeat the message with
disastrous results. I used to think that they were telling lies.
I can see now it was just crossed wires. This happened on
several occasions and gave rise to a bit of trouble. I don't
think it would happen now because I can communicate so
much better, and they have all learned to face me when
they speak to me.

I was not too popular at home either on certain evenings. Every week our church members attended meetings
for prayer and Bible study. These meetings were held in
various homes. The idea was that a small group of about ten
or twelve people would meet regularly in a family setting,
relax and get to know each other well. There were many
such meetings held every week around the town. One of
them was held in my parents' home. Each week the same
group of people would arrive to pray and study. I did not go
to this. I carried on with my hobbies or did homework or
played around with my brothers. This is where the trouble
began. I was so noisy around the house. I used to run up
and down stairs making a tremendous noise. I was very tall
for my age and had huge feet and of course I couldn't hear a
thing. Some of the church members found it hard to
concentrate with so much noise, because not only was I
stamping around, I was also often calling out far too loudly
to my brother. I must have been hard to cope with.

At the fellowship meetings with the youth group I had
my own problems. To begin with, for quite a long time, no
one knew how to respond to me. I was just left to sit there
and do the best I could. I found prayer meetings particularly hard to bear. Some people buried their heads in their
hands when they prayed. This meant I could not lip read
them. Others would speak or pray with barely any lip
movement and were impossible to follow. Sometimes I
could not see that anyone was speaking. I would suddenly
say something and find that I'd interrupted them.

When we were having a time of praying I would concentrate very hard to watch who was praying and to lip read the
prayers, so that I could join in. To do this I sat, naturally,

with my eyes open throughout the prayers. This made me fidgety. Sometimes I would drop my Bible or pen. My papers would rustle. Without realising it at all I was a noisy member of the group. My friends did not like to say anything. They knew it must be difficult for me. But they were only human and gradually these little things niggled them and some of them found it hard having me there. But now over the years we have ironed out most of these difficulties and the young people are very caring and understanding.

Perhaps the most upsetting incident with the youth group happened when I was sixteen. We had been invited by a church at Margate to go over one Sunday to help them with an evangelistic mission they'd been taking during the week. We were to take part in an open air service on the beach. Some of the group were also going to act some lively little plays to present the Gospel in a new way. To begin with everything went well. We travelled down through the lovely Kentish countryside enjoying the excitement of an outing together. On our way we picked up a hitch-hiker and gave him a lift for several miles. I could not take part in the conversation with him because everyone talked at once and didn't bother to explain anything to me. When we arrived at Margate I was already feeling isolated. We parked outside a small church and immediately joined the Margate fellowship on the beach for the open air service. I could see that the organisers had erected loudspeakers, but I could not work out how the power got to them. I looked around and was able to track a long wire to a car battery which was earthed in the sand. I could not hear it, but judging by the way people were listening it was working well. A loudspeaker is impossible to lip read so I moved to where I could see the preacher clearly. Many people who were out on the beach watched us singing and praying.

As I stood there on the sand it brought back to my memory things I'd heard about the school for the deaf in Margate. At my boarding school, although we'd never met anyone from the Margate school, we used to imagine what they were like. Being unkind schoolchildren we used to say they must be like animals. Now, standing there, looking out to sea I remembered these sad thoughts again. Later I was to meet some of the pupils and teachers from the Margate school, at the Crystal Palace deaf athletics. I found out how very nice they all were. Nowadays, I still like them, though I've never seen the school.

Fun and games on the beach followed the service. I enjoyed this as I could feel part of the group again. Tea came next, then a big prayer meeting to prepare for the evening service. All of our group who were going to act in the plays were feeling nervous about performing in front of a large congregation. Soon it was time to go to the Anglican church where we were helping with the service. After the acting, the service went on and on. This part was nothing to do with us. I got very bored. I saw many people get up and leave the church to go home. Some of them asked the vicar how much longer it was going to carry on, and he told them that he could not help it being so long. He thought it would be about another ten minutes. But it went on much longer. By now I was really fed up.

At last when we got out of the church, a friend John and I went to a fish and chip shop. I was starving and wanted some chips. Our leader Barry told us not to be too long and to come back to the mini-bus when we were ready. It was now quite late and there was the long journey back to Tunbridge Wells to make. There were two vehicles to take us home, the mini-bus and a car. It was at this point that misunderstandings arose and the evening's trouble began.

I had been told that as I had travelled down to Margate in the mini-bus, it was my turn to travel back in the car. It was only fair to give someone else a turn. Everyone preferred travelling in the mini-bus because it was more of a crowd and fun. But because I did not work and was not due at school the next day, I thought it a better idea to let one of the younger ones who was tired take my place in the car. I could then travel home more slowly in the mini-bus. I sent a message to say this to Barry the leader. He was anxious to be off. Now I thought that both the car and the mini-bus should have travelled home together in case of a break down. This is done now but was not planned for that night. So I wasted time up by the chip shop to make sure the car left before me. Others wanted to stay late in Margate too, but it was wrong of us all to want that.

While I was eating my chips I saw someone call me to go into the car. For reasons of his own, Barry did not like my idea of returning in the mini-bus. Looking back now I can see that he was concerned to get a large group of teenagers all safely home and in one piece. There was not room for individuals to start demanding what they wanted. At the time I thought he was being unkind. So I stayed at the shop door for a bit longer. Barry and Sue, a very petite and dainty girl, and deputy leader of the youth group, came up the road to me. 'Hurry up, Phillip,' they said, 'we are waiting to go. Come and get into the car.' As I have said, I had made up my mind not to go back in the car. I wanted to go back in the mini-bus. They tried to pull me, but I shoved them away. I got very angry with them.

Suddenly I went mad. I pulled Martin Chapman's hair and threw Sue against the shop window. Once more they tried to persuade me. Then they prayed and placed their hands on me. Because they would not understand my message that I wanted to go home in the mini-bus I thought they were not speaking the truth to me. I felt it was not right of them to tell lies. So I turned away and faced the shop door. Someone tried to pull me again but the power of the devil came in me. By now I was very upset. I felt a painful power of evil rise in me. I got stronger and felt I would be the most powerful man ever. I damaged the shop door handle. I was amazed at my strength. Without seeming to do anything, I bent the handle up. Roughly I pushed the others away and walked down the road towards the car. Everyone was relieved thinking I was calmly going to get in. But when I walked past the mini-bus, past the car and on down the road, consternation broke out. I did not look back. Barry called to some of the young people to stop me.

I ran off and shouted that I would make my own way home.
Barry ran into a pub to try to ring my father, but could not
get through.

I carried on running very fast. I crossed roads and passed
many people. When Barry heard that I'd disappeared from
sight he sent more people after me. I meanwhile ran on and
on, off into the dark, taking turnings to left and right. I
came to roads where there were no street lamps, and lost
my pursuers easily. I looked back and saw that no one was
in sight. Then I ran again, waited and ran again, hid by a car
and waited, waited. Suddenly I saw Andy Clarke, the
tallest boy in our group, run down the hill but he didn't turn
into the road where I was hiding. So I ran and ran and
climbed over a small fence and went into the corner of a
flat. Nobody could either see or hear me there. I was in the
darkest place. The place of the devil. I laughed silently with
the devil. Then I hid there for about five minutes. The devil
told me that they were all out hunting for me. Ha! Ha! Ha!

But I was frightened. I was worried and nervous of the
devil. I was still waiting and hoping that someone would
come, but no one came. Suddenly the devil went. Later,
the young people told me that some of them had been
praying for me in the mini-bus. It must have been while
they were praying for me that the devil left me. I felt
worried about what I'd done. I walked out of the dark
place. I walked along the road and finally joined a larger
road with street lights. I thought to myself, 'I must go back.
I must find the others, to go home. If I run away now, then
I'll never return home.'

I was feeling very mixed up. As you can see, sometimes I
went my own way. I didn't want to carry on living like that.
It was as if I was leading a double life with Christ. Sometimes I followed him and obeyed him and at other times I
did evil things. It was not until about a year later that I was
able to sort myself out and commit myself completely to
Christ. Up until then I was still in a mess.

So I walked along roads, until I saw Dave coming up to
me. I've never been so glad to see anyone in my life. I went

up to him. As soon as I met him I said I was sorry. He said he was sorry and we made it up. He said a prayer and I asked Jesus to rule in my heart again, not the devil. But I was still feeling very sad, and drained from my experience. When we got back to the others I got quietly into the mini-bus, the car had long since driven off, and we went home.

I cannot remember very much about the journey back, but I was feeling very subdued. Most of the young people did not understand me at that time. We all appeared foolish to each other. Now, years later, we understand each other well, and if I thought they were not speaking the truth or were misrepresenting me, I would be brave and speak to them from the Bible. When we finally got home I could see the light still on downstairs. My father was obviously waiting up for me. The mini-bus drove off and my father opened the door.

'Are you all right?' he asked me. I told him that I was, just about, and he told me to go on up to bed. As he did not say anything, I thought that he did not know anything about the evening's escapade. 'And there's no need for him ever to know,' I thought to myself. So I went up to bed. Early next morning I did not hear the phone ring. It was Barry's wife phoning my father to tell him in no uncertain terms all about my behaviour. When I came downstairs I had to face the music. How I hate telephones. How I wish leaders' wives could be cut off.

My father listened to what I had to say. 'The trouble with you,' he said, 'is that there's too much "I want," in your life. "I want to go in the mini-bus, I want this. I want that." No wonder you get into trouble. You must learn to ask for what you want more politely. You must not keep on and on about what you want all the time, and demand it. You must learn to say, "Please may I go back in the mini-bus," and if you are out with the group you must fit in with what the leaders say.'

I could see what Dad meant, but I hated having to be told all that. He said that I must visit Barry and his wife to apologise. So a few days later, I went round to have a talk. I was very sorry and ashamed of myself, for the way I'd been that Sunday night. We all prayed together and Barry talked to me, explaining passages from the Bible about love and discipline. He and Maureen his wife said of course they forgave me for being so difficult, for being rough with them and for running off, but that I would still have to be disciplined. I found this very hard to understand. Surely if they had forgiven me they should forget about that Sunday night? We should start again. Barry explained that it was only fair to everyone else that some discipline should be given. I was not at all happy about this.

When it was time to go to the next youth meeting, I went there rather cautiously. I was not sure how the young people would greet me. Some of them looked a bit worried when I got there. They wanted to know what was going to happen about the Sunday night. I went up to the ones who had been at Margate with me and apologised to them, and we all made it up. Maureen was running the evening and she announced to everyone that she and Barry had talked to me about my behaviour and it was all forgiven. She said she did not want anyone else to go on talking about it. Then came the bombshell. Although I was forgiven, she explained that as a discipline I would not be allowed to go on the next outing. How unfair! 'Oh no!' I called out. She took no notice of me and carried on leading the meeting.

Later, during the break for refreshments I tackled her in the kitchen. 'God forgives and forgets,' I stormed at her. 'How can you punish me like this.' Quietly but firmly Maureen told me that the decision was final and that I would have to accept it. When I went home my father had been warned that I was angry. He of course backed up Maureen and Barry. When I discovered that the outing I was to miss was the best outing of the year, a barbecue on the beach, I was very fed up.

What also worried me was in case I should get involved in another terrible escapade like Margate. I still thought it had happened in some way because someone had misunderstood the message I'd sent to Barry. Say it happened again? I resolved it shouldn't. I resolved to remain silent. I was greatly helped at this time by some verses in the Psalms which I read. David had felt just like me.

I am like a deaf man, who cannot hear, like a mute, who
    cannot open his mouth;
I have become like a man who does not hear, whose mouth
    can offer no reply.
I wait for you, O Lord; you will answer, O Lord my God.
For I said, 'Do not let them gloat or exalt themselves over
    me when my foot slips.'

For I am about to fall, and my pain is ever with me.
I confess my iniquity; I am troubled by my sin.
Many are those who are my vigorous enemies;
Those who hate me without reason are numerous.
Those who repay my good with evil slander me when I
    pursue what is good.

O Lord, do not forsake me; be not far from me, O my God.
Come quickly to help me, O Lord my Saviour.
(Psalm 38: 13–22)

A few lines of the next psalm summed up my feelings very well at this time.

I said, 'I will watch my ways and keep my tongue from sin;
I will put a muzzle on my mouth as long as the wicked are in
    my presence.'
But when I was silent and still, not even saying anything
    good, my anguish increased.
My heart grew hot within me, and as I meditated, the fire
    burned; then I spoke with my tongue.
(Psalm 39: 1–2)

In the Good News version I like the words, 'I kept quiet, not saying a word, not even about anything good. But my suffering only grew worse.'

How I resolved this and how all the members of the youth group gradually became my very best friends, I will tell in a later chapter. For now a big event was looming up in my life. It was time to leave home again and go to college.

12. College Days

After the excitement of winning the gold medal at Birmingham I left school, looking forward to college life.

But first came the holidays. It was a busy summer with a week in Bournemouth with the family followed by a youth camp near Bath. This was a new experience for me. There was a service every evening and there were strict camp rules. For example no smoking was allowed and it was forbidden for boys to go into girls' tents or girls into boys' tents. If these rules were broken you could be sent home immediately with no warning given. As far as I was concerned these rules were fine. It was a Christian camp and I expected them. Some of the young people found it a bit too strict I think. Every morning and afternoon we had fun and games or went out visiting places of interest. It was during the evening sessions that I found I was having a struggle with the Lord. I was not finding being a Christian very easy. My life was not very much better than before. I was only booked into this camp for a week but I made a mental note to go back for two weeks the following year. Perhaps with two weeks' study I would come to grips with being a Christian. I returned from camp, the spiritual side not having made much impact on me. I was not in the strongest position to face the difficulties and temptations which lay ahead of me.

My parents drove me over to college one beautiful September Sunday. We unloaded my cases and were shown where to take them. Suddenly I saw some of the deaf students using sign language. I had not used it for years and years, and had forgotten it completely. Since I'd become a

Christian I'd made a special effort with my speech as that
would allow me to talk to anybody, whereas sign language
limits you to talking only to people who know it. I tried to
speak to them without signing but they did not understand
me very well. I felt disheartened at this beginning to college
life. My parents were soon ready to drive home. They
waved to me as they drove off. My father said, 'Be a good
boy. Remember, Jesus is with you, and we'll see you on
Friday evening.' I watched their car disappear and turned
into the building feeling sad and lonely. I unpacked my
clothes and books in my own study bedroom and settled in
as best I could.

The next day I began to see how college was different
from school. We had to sort out which subjects we would be
taking for 'O' level and then we were free for the rest of the
day. I immediately had an argument with the staff over
which subjects I could study. They would only allow me to
take three 'O' level subjects, maths, technical drawing and
art.

I suddenly felt very homesick and lonely. What could I
do for the rest of the day? I had got on quite well with some
of the other students I'd talked to, but now I wanted to be
on my own. I also wanted to escape from so many new
faces. I got on my bike and cycled off. I rode a long way,
further and further from college, to drive the loneliness
away. I cycled about fifteen miles and tried to visit some
friends who live in Sutton, but they were not in. Now I had
to cycle back again with no cup of tea to help me. When I
was about five miles from college something went wrong
with my gears. I was only able to get into fifth gear as I was
going up a hill. This made it too hard to ride as I needed to
be in first gear for hills. I got off my bike and looked to see
what had happened and found that a wire had broken at the
gear switch. I could not mend it. I tried the third gear and
found I could still use that, but I was much slower coming
home than I had planned. At last I arrived back in college in
time for tea, and asked a third year student to come and
look at my bike. He came from Scotland. He told me that I

must buy a new wire in the bike shop which was somewhere in the town centre about two or three miles away. I couldn't face any more cycling that day but decided tomorrow would do.

The next few weeks were not easy. To begin with I didn't bother to do much Bible study and my faith sank lower and lower. The other students, when they discovered that I was a Christian, teased me and made fun of me. They tried to show me bad things and make me do things wrong for Christians to do. Because my own faith was weak, I led a double life. I talked about it to my father and he explained how at home I was surrounded by Christians and Christian standards. At college it was different. I was in the minority. I must choose firmly which way I wanted to go and stand up to the other students. I was missing friends from home because over the summer holiday while I'd been away I'd been so wrapped up in thinking about college that I had got out of touch. Now I was away at college I didn't have the time to write and at weekends it was not easy to get back into the swim of things with them.

Back at college I tried to speak to some of the others about Christ and teach them the words of the Lord, and the law of God, but I didn't do it very well. I was worried that the other students would think I was proud, but I tried to share my faith with them. It was not much good though because I was so muddled up in myself. In many ways I was not very friendly with the other students and was always trying to do better than them. And unfortunately I still had the odd fight!

We were kept busy at college with plenty of football. I enjoyed this as it helped me to keep fit. However much of a mess I made of my Christian life at this time I can say that I always did my best for the Lord in sports. I did not feel that I was ever doing it to please the teachers or the team or the school, but the Lord. In the Bible it says, 'Whatever you do, work at it with all your heart, as working for the Lord, not for men' (Col. 3:23).

Not all our lessons were taken at the small college for

deaf students. Every day we went to another large technical college at Weybridge where we joined with hearing students in various studies. This was a good idea as it meant although we had the help of the staff at the deaf college, we were still mixing with the outside world for part of each day. It was during these lessons that I made good friends with another deaf boy, John.

Not that all the lecturers at Weybridge were very suitable for teaching deaf students. We found one woman teacher whom we had every Monday, particularly difficult to lip read. She had grey hair and long front teeth. This affected her speech so that we could never understand her. Because of this we got bored and didn't even bother to work. Sometimes we didn't even bother to copy from the blackboard. We just talked and joked.

Another teacher, while we were copying from the blackboard, would sometimes bang our desks and say, 'Look at me. I want to talk to everyone.' We would look up and listen and follow what he was saying. Then he would suddenly forget that he'd got deaf pupils in with the other students, and turn and face the blackboard. We would assume that he had finished speaking to us and would put our heads down and get on with our work. We could not hear that he was still explaining something. The teacher of course had not finished. When he turned round and saw that we were not attending he would tap John on the arm to attract his attention who in turn would tap Peter's arm who in turn would tap my arm. By this time all the other students were laughing. The teacher thought we were playing him up deliberately. We liked his lessons, but sometimes our eyes got tired from lip reading for so long and then our attention would wander and we'd get bored. 'Come on. Wake up!' he would shout at us.

Another hazard we had to cope with was teachers with beards. It is impossible to lip read a person with a large and woolly beard. You cannot see the lips. All you can see is the tongue and the beard going up and down!

Our art teacher didn't have a beard, but he didn't open

his mouth wide enough. I did not like his lips because none of the deaf students could understand what he was saying. He used to get angry all the time and pressed his 2B pencil hard on to the paper when he was worked up. He did not have a very easy time with us because he had two rooms, sometimes three, to look after at the same time. Whenever he was in one the students in the other room would talk and stop working. Then he would rush back in and get angry with us. He finally came up with what he thought was a brilliant idea. He split the three deaf pupils up into separate rooms. Now we could not be a nuisance. But we soon worked our way round that. John would say he was coming downstairs to the toilet but really he just came down to talk to me. I would go up to John's room and pretend I needed my pencil sharpening. All I was looking for was a chance to talk to John again. No we didn't make life easy for the poor art teacher.

Life at college was not all lessons of course. During Monday to Thursday we had private study, when we could work either in our bedrooms or our classrooms, whichever we liked. Sometimes when we didn't have much to do we just enjoyed talking with each other up in our rooms. There were three of us, John, Peter and I who got on well and we always had plenty to discuss. Sometimes we would stay talking in our rooms when we were meant to be downstairs in a classroom. On these occasions a teacher would come looking for us. We could not hear footsteps. Our only hope was that someone would see a teacher approaching. Whenever we were warned that trouble was coming I used to rush and hide in the toilet until the teacher had gone. Once the coast was clear we would carry on talking. We all had so much to talk about and there was never enough time, especially as I went home every weekend, or away to stay with my aunt at Epsom. Other students who lived a long way away had to stay there all the time.

Gradually as the first year went by things got worse for me at college, as I frequently spoke very rudely to members of staff. The main trouble was through our computer lessons which were held at the deaf college. I was in a small group in the top set. Our teacher taught us very very slowly with far too much explanation, and we could see that we would never get through the course. We would all have preferred to get on with using the computer. Instead we had to copy pages of work from the blackboard, and got very frustrated. We knew that the teacher was only copying out of a text book. Why couldn't he photocopy it and give us all a sheet to save so much work? Chris who was in our class used to play up very badly. In almost every lesson he would sit down at his table, then he would look up at the clock. Throughout the entire lesson he would watch it all the time the teacher was talking to us. Minute by minute, hour by hour, second by second he would go on watching, watching. This used to anger the teacher who would try to get Chris to do some work.

Sometimes I was so bored with the easy work I would cry out, 'Oh, this is so easy, and very boring. Why don't you do something better for us? We all understand this work and it's boring.' The teacher got cross with me but he never changed the type of work we were doing. So I told him again and asked the students whether they found the lessons boring and easy. They all agreed that they were boring. I wondered what we could do instead of the computer lessons. I had the idea of having Bible studies but that was rather a wild idea!

During a later lesson I told the teacher again how boring we found the lessons. This time he reported me to the senior tutor. He gave me an interview in his room. I thought he might be going to boot me out of college. I bravely tried to explain to him what the root of the problem was, because I wanted to get the course changed for all of us. He explained that it would not be possible to change the course and that I must watch my behaviour. I left his room feeling very sad that I had failed.

One day I thought I might get into big trouble, perhaps be killed or jailed for life. I thought it would be better if I were to leave college and mix with Christians again who could help me live a better life. If I were with Christians more often I would have more time praying and praising God. But I felt too that I must work harder at college and do better there. I wanted to forget many of the bad words I'd learned at college. I wanted more wisdom and a deeper Christian faith.

One evening I was alone in my study bedroom, feeling very lonely. I decided to read the Bible so I got it out and read it for a long time. This was the time I was wondering how to write songs and music, with no idea how to begin.

I found some words in the back of my old Bible which said, 'The step to heaven'. I tried to understand it but there seemed to be more than one step. I found the index in the Good News Bible and looked up the word heaven: 'abode of God, angels and blessed dead. OT Genesis 28:12, 17.' I looked this reference up in the Good News Bible. 'He dreamt that he saw a stairway reaching from earth to heaven, with angels going up and coming down on it.' It was Jacob's dream at Bethel. 'He was afraid and said, "What a terrifying place this is! It must be the house of God; it must be the gate that opens into heaven."'

Suddenly the idea came to me that I might write a song called, 'The Way to Heaven'. I looked up other verses on other pages, because I wanted my song to be only words from the Bible. I wanted to copy words and sentences down and rearrange them into a song.

I was absorbed in doing this when suddenly another student came into my room flashing his torch. He was a third year student. He asked me a question but while he was talking to me he saw my Bible and the song.

'Do you know about Jesus?' he asked me.

'Yes,' I answered.

'And are you a Christian?' he asked.

I said yes again. He was very pleased and sat down on the bed and told me all about his life. He told me how he had become a Christian between the ages of eight and twelve. He talked to me a lot about God, Jesus and the Bible. I had not realised that he was a Christian until then. I was very pleased with his visit and asked him if he knew of any other Christians in college. To my surprise he mentioned several names.

'We have a Christian Union here once or twice a week. It is held in my bedroom from nine in the evening until ten o'clock.' He talked to me for about twenty minutes until he had to leave to visit someone else. I was very interested in everything he'd said to me and carried on writing my song until late into the night. I kept thinking about Jesus and the Bible and I prayed much longer than usual. Suddenly I went off to sleep.

After this I joined in occasional meetings with the Christian Union and found them a help to me, but other interests frequently took over. Football was one of them and sometimes I went to see my favourite team Tottenham Hotspur play. I did this at weekends when I stayed at college or when I was at my aunt's. I travelled by train up to Waterloo station and from there by Underground to Liverpool Street, where I changed trains for White Hart Lane. From that station it was a five or ten minute walk to Spurs football ground.

On the journey back from the match it was always very crowded on the trains. The platforms were packed with people going back into London. Once I noticed that as the train drew in there were only a few people in the carriage. One of them was reading a newspaper and he did not see the crowds on the platform. His eyes nearly popped out of his head when the carriage suddenly filled to overflowing. Another woman stared in amazement at the crowd.

I often took my friend John with me up to matches. We had some difficulty in getting through the crowds on the way home. Because I was so tall I was able to push my way through the crush. The entry was on the left and I managed to squeeze in. John was swept along past the entrance to the second gate. John pushed his way in but got stuck behind another man. To his surprise a huge policeman grabbed his coat and pulled him along the wall to help him get into the station. John looked tired from the struggle and a bit shocked at the way the policeman had pulled him.

We enjoyed the journey back. We were right at the back of the train in the end coaches. When the train stopped at some of the smaller stations the last coach did not reach the platform. One of the Spurs supporters tried to get out but he couldn't because he would have had to get out in the tunnel. We lip read another man telling them to pull the alarm unless he fancied jumping from the moving train when we moved up. He added another joke which I didn't catch but everyone in the coach laughed. Fortunately the train moved slowly and stopped again so that the people in the last coach could get out. It was on that journey that a boy who could not find a seat climbed up on to the luggage rack and lay down there, as if he were in bed. I thought it looked too high to be comfortable but he didn't seem to mind. Another funny thing happened to two people who were busy talking to each other. They had counted how many stops there were on their journey before they need get out. The train stopped once at a red light and went on again to a station. These people kept on talking and didn't look out of the window. When the train had stopped the right number of times, they jumped out on to the platform. Suddenly they saw the name of the station and jumped quickly back in again. They had got out one stop too soon. How we all laughed.

Apart from watching professional football we played in our own five-a-side football league at Staines sports centre. It was held indoors in a very small hall so the pitch was not full sized, and the game was much faster. I was goal keeper and enjoyed saving the ball. We used to play many other teams and generally ended up about eighth or ninth in the league out of sixteen teams. We used to play every Thursday evening in the winter and during the break between games we used to go over to a nearby pub, not to drink beer, just cola. We made sure not to drink too much as we had to be ready for the next match. It was warm and cosy in the pub and we enjoyed having time to talk.

We sometimes found it hard when playing hearing

teams, because we could not hear the whistle.

I still wasn't very good at keeping out of trouble. One day during the last art lesson before the exams John and I went to the store room. I forget what it was that John was looking for. I saw a box of a hundred pencils. What would I want with a hundred pencils? But I took the box and rolled it up in John's art papers. Then we went off. John wanted to know why we were hurrying away. Suddenly the art teacher saw us rushing down the stairs. He had heard us rattling the pencils! We ran outside but a few minutes later we were caught and the teacher searched my rucksack, but there was nothing there. Then he found the pencils, stuffed inside my jumper. We were taken into another room where he phoned the head of our college for the deaf. I had to write an explanation and I admitted that I had stolen the pencils. 'It was all my fault, truly,' I wrote. I thought about what I'd done and decided that I would try hard not to be a trouble-maker any more. I said I was sorry to the Lord and he forgave my sin. As a punishment I was sent home from college for several days.

What pain that must have caused my parents. But that is all over now. I do not think about it any more and John and I are happy now that we behave well.

And so my first year at college ended. It had not been very good and three times the senior tutor warned me about my behaviour. If I were not careful I should be expelled.

I was glad that the summer holidays were approaching.

13. Something Special

As I had planned, I returned to the Bath youth camp for two weeks. It was to be an eventful time for me. In fact it was great. On the first night I slept in a tent with some other boys, but there was not enough room for me. The next day I asked a boy if I could borrow his small tent to sleep in by myself for the next two weeks. He said it would be all right and he put it up for me. It suddenly occurred to me that if I were on my own I would have problems waking up in the morning. An alarm clock is no good to a deaf person! This concerned me so I prayed seriously that the Holy Spirit would wake me in the mornings.

Although at this camp we went on outings and enjoyed ourselves together, it is the spiritual side which I remember most. That night after the evening meeting, I had something hot to eat then went to bed and prayed again about waking up in the morning. So I went to sleep. When I awoke I found my watch and looked at the time. It was half past six. The Holy Spirit had woken me and I felt different from the way I normally feel when I wake on my own. I thought, 'Thank you God for waking me up, with all my heart. What a beautiful morning. How beautiful it is. How beautiful, like heaven. Thank you God for waking me up. Praise the Lord with all my heart.'

Then I got ready for a wash and a shave. Bother. I did not like having to shave but it has to be done every morning. I was so moved by the experience of being awakened early that I wrote a song about it.

When I went to a youth camp
In Bath for two weeks, on the
Second night, I slept in a small
Tent on my own, but I could not
Get up by myself in the morning
Because I am deaf. I had no alarm
Clocks but I prayed to God to wake
Me up in the morning. Then I went to sleep.

Next morning I woke up by the Holy
Spirit. I looked at my watch and
It said, half past six. So I praised
The Lord and I thank you God for
Waking me up.

Chorus
Thank you God for waking me
Up. What a beautiful morning.
Beautiful it is. How beautiful
It is. Very beautiful like heaven.
Thank you God for waking me up.
Praise the Lord O my soul.

Apart from one morning when I slept on until half past
eight after a very tiring day the day before, I woke early
every morning of the camp. This was something very
special for me. Every night we had a meeting in the big tent.
Pastor Mike Godward spoke to us. Someone used to write
down for me a list of the important things he said. On one
occasion he said that there would be a time for everyone to
join in and share what Christ had done for them in their
lives. I tried hard to follow what he meant by this. Afterwards I asked someone to read out my message when I had
written it down. As far as I can remember, I wrote roughly
the following:

I am with Jesus, yesterday today and forever, just as you
are. I love you but I understand if some of you do not like

me, but I love you. In my tent I slept there every night on my own. No one woke me up in the mornings. It was the Holy Spirit who woke me up. I am deaf and I cannot hear you. I do not want to hear again, from the age of five until I go to heaven. I have been prayed for many times, but it will not work while I am on the earth. That is I cannot hear you, but I can hear God from you.

Many Christians were amazed and moved by what I said and thought it was very good. During the meeting I felt God was speaking to me in a special way. He was telling me to write a book about my life. This seemed impossible. It was the hardest thing the Holy Spirit has ever urged me to do. Part of me felt elated, filled with the Spirit. 'Oh Lord, it must be the hand of the Lord on me. When I start to write this book I will not be the author, as I cannot write neither can I remember the whole part of my life.' It seemed an exciting job but at the same time a difficult one to do.

After the meeting I went up to talk to Pastor Mike Godward. I told him that the Lord had told me to write a book. He looked at me and said, 'Are you going to do it?'

'Yes!' I answered.

'Hallelujah!' he exclaimed. He did not tell anyone else and I am very glad that I was able to tell him.

The two weeks of camp rushed by and did not seem very long to me. I enjoyed it very much and some of the young people asked me if I would be willing to come the following year. I said that perhaps I might.

On the last day of camp I waited for my parents to come and pick me up. They came with my two brothers and looked round the camp site. Then we all set off for our family holiday.

During our two weeks' holiday in Devon, I started to write in a little rough book, jotting down some of the memories I could recall. I carried on writing when I got home and at the end of three weeks I had finished. But all that I had managed to write were fifty-nine pages. I thought it was impossible to make a long story out of my life. I could only write a little. When I had thought about it some more I bought a larger-sized note book and wrote it out again adding more stories as I remembered them. Little did I realise how long it would take until it would be finally finished and ready for the publisher. As to who would publish it I had no idea.

The camp at Bath had been a great experience and I had learned a lot. People sometimes ask me whether I find it hard to praise God. I suppose they mean is it hard to praise him when I have to suffer the handicap of being deaf. I don't see it like that, and I don't find it hard to praise him. I don't use music as it is no help, as I cannot hear it. I feel nothing through music. Worship is like a doxology, time to consider the blessings of God. I see with my eyes and feel with my heart. Sometimes my heart is joyful. Sometimes it hurts me when I look around and think about what I see. I pray in my mind most of the time as it is private. I can see Jesus and it isn't hard to praise God.

The very day after I got back from my holidays I had to go back to college. Oh, no! What a shock. It can't be good to go back the very next day. But that is life and I had had a good break.

14. Farewell to College

I returned to college for my second year, determined to behave better and to work harder and as a result things went well. I was in the same study bedroom as before. Every night I worked there on my new book. I don't think I told anyone what I was doing. Part of me was excited about doing it and part of me was shy. On the first page I wrote about my birth and early life but naturally I could not remember much about that. I did not find the actual writing too difficult. I had read a book called *Tell my People I Love Them* by Clifford Hill. In it I read, 'When the hand of the Lord comes upon me I am thinking quite clearly, but I am not aware of what the next sentence will be. I simply write down the words as they come into my head.' (page 63)

I found that it was like that with me. I did not have any strong feelings. I just sat and wrote and memories came back to me. It may surprise some people that I have been so open about my life and my bad behaviour. I had been reading Nicky Cruz's book *Run Baby Run*. In this book I saw how Nicky's life was changed by Christ and I thought if I was truthful and shared what my life was really like and showed how Christ eventually changed it, then readers too might be helped and they might see that Christ can help them. I did find that when I came to difficult bits to remember, the Holy Spirit helped me and brought back memories. The hardest part I found to write about was my first year at college. I think that was because the experiences were still too close to me. It is easier to write about events that are further away.

I had to fit my book writing in with my college studies,

but as the term progressed I found time to write some more songs. I enjoyed this and soon had written more than a dozen. I also had fun making a music programme for the computer. Not of course that I could hear it when it was played.

As with any college most of the social life centred on the students' common room. In our second year we had a new one, larger than the old one and with new furniture, television and video and a new snooker table, and darts boards etc. We all liked it. The old common room had got very knocked about with our rough treatment and the staff told us to report anyone who damaged anything in the new room. Teenage boys can get very clumsy and start to fool around very easily without meaning to damage anything. One evening I was sitting in the common room with several others. There was a boy who was trying to tease another student. He ran and brought both feet off the ground like in karate. He flew through the air feet first. The other student dodged out of the way. There was a terrible crash and the boy's feet went straight through the wall. He rushed outside to see if the outer wall was damaged but fortunately it was only the inner wall. One of the teachers who was in the adjacent computer room heard the noise and ran out and caught the trouble-maker.

Afterwards when John, Peter and I were talking about the incident and laughing about it we imagined what would have happened if he had hit the wall much harder. Say he had gone right through the common room wall and the computer room wall and arrived feet first by the teacher. He would have looked up with bricks and rubble on his head, his hair covered in dust and his eyebrows looking wild. The student would have got up and said, 'Oh, sorry Sir.' and the teacher's eyes would have gone round and round.

Another messy accident occurred when I was in the kitchen with John. He decided he'd like to see how the fire extinguisher worked. It was a special one for kitchen use with electrical equipment. So he pressed the button just a little. Suddenly white powder flew out all over the place. John tried to fiddle with the button to stop it but more and more powder poured out thickly smothering everything. John tried to get it over to the sink which soon filled up. At last the extinguisher ran out of powder. The mess was terrible. The kitchen looked like a snow scene. I tried to help him clear up but it was difficult to get rid of. The powder clogged the sink and it would not wash away. I put a bucket under the sink and undid the pipe. Water and powder gushed out. When the bucket was full I put the pipe back and threw the powder away. Then I did the same again until the sink was cleared. Poor John had to pay towards a new extinguisher which cost about seventy pounds.

John was always a great talker and was always full of ideas. He had great plans for rebuilding our bedrooms so that we all had more space. He also wanted his own bathroom as he objected to queuing up every morning for his wash.

Not all our activities had such disastrous results. Bikes were very popular and every day nearly all the students cycled the three miles to Weybridge to the tech. There was one hazard in the college grounds, a rose bed. During the autumn when it was windy the rose thorns fell on to the path. As a result students were forever getting punctures. When I saw what was happening I took great care to avoid the danger.

One student had a motor bike and another a car. We cyclists always used to say that it wasn't fair for them to have such an easy way to get to college. But we enjoyed racing them every day. We frequently beat the car which often got caught in traffic jams while we sped past. It was harder to beat the motor bike which could weave in and out of the traffic and make a very good speed. It added excitement to each day to have this race to see who was the first deaf student to arrive.

Apart from the daily ride to Weybridge, on the long summer evenings when we had time between tea and study period John, Peter, David and I enjoyed going out for long rides.

We went out searching for the longest downhill stretch of road. We finally found a good hill about two miles away. It was a private road, well made up with no potholes. We enjoyed coasting down this hill getting faster and faster. We only braked if a car came, which was not often. The other thing we had to be careful of was flying golf balls as the lane crossed a golf course at the bottom. The lane led on to a main road but before that we had to sail over a ramp about fifty metres from the junction. It was a most enjoyable ride down. The only problem was the ride back to college along the main road which included seven hills.

We often went out to that spot. Once I set off down hill ahead of John. After about half a minute I looked back to see if he was coming. He was not in sight. I waited and still he didn't come. So I left my bike and walked back up the hill to find him. There he was off his bike, hurt. The front brake had worked loose and fallen into the wheel which had locked, throwing John off the bike. We tried bending the bike back into shape and John found he could still cycle it carefully as long as he didn't try to go round corners. We managed to get back to college safely though I looked back every ten seconds to check that he was still coming.

Suddenly time flew by and there were only four months to go before leaving. These last months were not without trouble. Various things were stolen at college and other things were vandalised. Because of my past history the chairman of our student council, David, asked me whether I had got anything to do with it. He was only doing what he had to do. I was able quite truthfully to tell him that I was not the culprit. He asked me several times more but I gave him the same answer. I did not know who had done it either. I asked him whether I could help in any way in tracking down the guilty people. I was good at tracking people. As I explained in an earlier chapter I tracked my girl friend home on many occasions.

John, Peter and I decided to have a secret meeting to

discuss the trouble and to work out what we could do about it. We were sure it had something to do with some ex-schoolboys from a nearby school who had been allowed to stay in our college. I saw someone acting suspiciously that very day and reported him.

I did not enjoy the last term. I was hit by someone on my cheek again and it hurt badly. This happened twice in football matches. I was sent to hospital again for an X-ray but nothing had happened to the bone. The circulation was not very good and the doctor told me not to get hit there any more.

At last my final exams were taken. I attempted 'A' level technical drawing and 'O' level maths and added maths, all of which I am pleased to say I passed.

One of the favourite songs I had written that term was entitled 'Farewell College' and it seems a good idea to end this chapter with it.

Farewell College

Farewell college, I am going now to worship the Lord
Farewell college, I'm going out in joy,
Farewell college, its hard work ends
Because of work I've had not time
To worship the Lord.
They fasted and prayed and placed their hands on me.
Farewell college. I'm going now to worship the Lord.

Chorus
Farewell college, farewell college, farewell college
Farewell college, farewell college, farewell college
Farewell, farewell, farewell college
Now I am going out in joy.

I love them all and say goodbye to everyone at college
I must not cry and cry but go and worship the Lord.
Hope they say farewell to me

Hope not to lose the sign language of the deaf to the
   hearing
Now I am going out in joy.

Chorus   repeat

Farewell college, now that's all over
I must leave now. and find a job.
G...o...o...d...b...y...e!

15. Out to Work

For some months before leaving college I had been thinking about what work I would do. I talked to the careers officer to discuss full-time work with him. He suggested that as I was interested in computers I should try to become a computer operator first. When I had been working for some years at that, I could become a computer programmer. They told me that I must not try to find a job on my own. They would find one for me. I said thank you very much.

I then typed out beautifully a letter of application, stating my education, my exam results, my hobbies and interests and the part-time work I had had so far. I explained I was deaf but that I could lip read. This letter I sent off to every notable firm in my home area.

The results were disappointing. Most answers told me that there were no vacancies. Others wanted higher qualifications. Several firms sent me a form to complete. One of these was the National Provident Institution where my father worked. By the time July came and I was due to leave college there was no job on the horizon.

Once I was home the excitement and relief at leaving college wore off a bit. But there was one good thing about all my spare time. I could carry on writing my book and also write more songs.

That summer there was a general election. I found it very interesting the way each candidate wanted us to vote for him. The idea came to me, 'Vote for Jesus'. I thought about it and imagined what could happen. Say for example the Labour Party candidate was to come to the door and tell us

all about the Labour policy. When we had listened then we
could tell him about the Jesus way and the Jesus policy for
his life. He would be amazed that such a life is a gift. After
talking about it he would walk back to the Labour head
office, would hand in his resignation and follow the Jesus
way. The same would happen to all the other candidates.
What a dream!

I wrote a song about the election, calling on every one to
vote for Jesus Christ Superstar. One of the verses went like
this:

> Remember I was saying to you to
> Vote for Jesus Christ.
> But I am not still waiting for
> Our party to win over the General Election
> But I know that the last will be the
> Winner. That's the Bible tells me so.
> The Bible tells me so.

Meanwhile I was still at home with no job. I filled in the
time helping my mother with housework. Useful to learn
cooking, washing and cleaning, in case I ever get a flat on
my own. I also helped my father at weekends up at the
allotment. I wondered how long it would be before I heard
about a job.

It was August again and one day the phone rang. It was a
man from my father's office. He asked whether I wanted a
job as a clerk. It would be temporary, for two or three
weeks. My father had taken the call and he explained it all
to me. 'Say, yes please,' I told him. So on the first Monday
in September I began work. I wondered how I would get on
and whether the other people in the office would understand me. The NPI building was huge with hundreds of
people working there. I would have to do well. A temporary job was a start but I was praying for a full-time job.
What hope was there for me? The unemployment figures
were rising every week. Many friends I knew were on the
dole. What chance was there for me as a deaf teenager to

get a full-time job? Surely a firm would always choose a
hearing candidate to whom they could talk easily? With
such thoughts in my head I put on the smart new suit my
parents had bought for me and began work.

On the first day the senior clerks showed me my work
which was very repetitive and quite easy to grasp. The
other people I worked with were kind and pleasant and if
the work got a bit boring they would tell jokes. The only
difficulty they had with me was when the phone on my desk
rang. I would carry on with my paper work, quite oblivious
of the noise!

At the end of my first fortnight the boss asked me if I
would stay for a third week. Meanwhile the manager
phoned my father to say that they were thinking of offering
me a full-time post, but that they would have to discuss it.
The government had a scheme to help school leavers get
work and they might employ me under those terms.

That weekend our church was having a series of special
meetings with a guest speaker. I spent a lot of time praying
about my future and the hopes of getting a permanent job.
It was a tremendous service and I felt the power of the Holy
Spirit there. After Charles Dross the speaker had finished
he asked anyone who wanted to become a Christian to
come forward to the stage, so that he could pray for them.
Next, Charles asked all of us to come out to surround them
with prayer and give them our support. There was a great
sense of praise and worship and freedom. I joined in
praising God and dancing with joy.

The next day the manager at work said that he and the
other managers had discussed me. They were pleased with
how hard I'd worked and how well I'd got on. They would
like to offer me a full-time job. Thank you Lord, thank you
for my new job. I praised him and was very happy for it.

Now I was busy every day. No time to get bored. I found
the job hard work. Part of it is to find files for members of
staff. I have to go up to the files in the roof, all two hundred
and fifty thousand of them!

To my delight I found that a member of our church youth

group Tim Ellwood was working in another department of NPI. We used to go out in our lunch hour together and I asked him to help me live a better life according to the Bible. Sometimes when I did not understand what he was saying we used to get wild with each other, but not for long. We were very good friends and did all sorts of things together. It was a great help to have another Christian working with me.

I was free during evenings and began writing more songs. I also went over my book with Tim and some other friends who helped correct some of my English as well as remind me of various incidents. One of the songs I wrote is called 'Amen'.

> Amen
> It is so or
> May it be so
> The faithful and
> True witness.
>
> Amen
> Who is the origin
> Of all that God
> Has created.
>
> Amen
> May it be so
> We pray every day with
> God, we shall
> Say
>
> Amen
> At the end of
> Praying every day
> Because it is so,
> May it be so.
>
> Thank you Lord
> Amen.

Now that I was at home I was able to get into a better routine of prayer and Bible reading. I spent about the same amount of time on each. I did not spend time asking God to heal my deafness, but I did frequently ask him to help me speak more clearly. The badly-formed speech of deaf people is one of the biggest hurdles to communication with others. I wanted to speak beautiful words to Christians as well as to non-Christians. Gradually my speech has improved though I still make mistakes. Sometimes I will shape my lips incorrectly and say the wrong sound. For example I might say, 'By bother bakes bacaroni' instead of 'My mother makes macaroni'. It is only when patient friends point this out that I can correct myself. I am rather at the stage of a foreigner who has learned English sufficiently well to get by. Very few people will actually correct him. But his English is far from perfect. It is a kindness to point out mistakes, however, and so I'm glad when my friends help me.

I think my favourite books in the Bible are the two books of Corinthians. They teach so much about Jesus, about loving one another and about the Holy Spirit. I read the Bible in various ways. Sometimes I study a special passage, or I may read a book all the way through. Sometimes I use notes to help me. I think it is important to read the Bible thoroughly and to use different methods so that the widest possible understanding can be gained.

Another bonus of being home was that I could join in with all the youth activities again. It was a time when we all got to know each other much better, even though it was not always easy. I was going through a time when I was very seriously and earnestly seeking to do God's will and wanting to study his word more and more. I wanted all the help I could get. Our leader was away in Africa for about five weeks and during his absence things got a bit slack. The young people did not always remember to help me by writing down headings in the sermons. When we had times of praising God they seldom shared with me what everyone was praying about. Sometimes the services seemed very long with too much music and nothing that I could join in with. Once again I had periods of getting bored, but even so I knew that at every meeting I saw Jesus there. I was getting so frustrated with the patchy help I was getting I worked out a system to ensure that each week someone was on duty to write notes for me. I wrote out a sheet of requirements and handed it round to everyone with a list of dates when they were to perform. I'm not called slave driver for nothing! The instructions I handed round read as follows:

The System
Please come and sit with me. Come by 10.00 a.m. Please do not be late. If you are right handed then please sit on the left side of me. For the left handers, please sit on the right side of me. If I do not come in the morning, then please still make notes for me. I will study it later.

Please make sure that you have got your pens. No pencils or red pens please.

Please do not make too many mistakes. If you do, do not worry. Please make a nice page for me so that I can understand it. If I point to a word it means I don't understand the meaning of the word. Please change it to another word. Please do not forget to number the pages.

Please write down all the prayers. Do not copy them from books but make up your own please.
Please write down most words that the minister says.
NO staring into space please. You will lose your place if you do.
Please do not talk to your friends or to others while doing this duty.

Please use simple words that I can understand.
Love Phillip   Vote for Jesus.

Warning If you are lazy then something will happen. Please do not let this happen.
For the cards with the dates on Please keep your card safe. Please put it on your bedroom wall. Please do not put it with your other things. Please let me know if you cannot come on that date. Tell me seven days before please. Otherwise see the warning note.

You may wonder whether I still had any friends left in the youth group after issuing such orders. All I can say is that the young people at my church are a very special bunch. They put up with me and all my ways. Although sometimes I sink into despair when they forget to share talks and studies with me we also have some good times and plenty of laughs together. I owe them all a lot.

While our youth leader was away I reached an all time low of desperation. Although I had handed out my instructions and given people the dates in good time some of them let me down. I couldn't believe it. Even my best friend Tim suddenly said that he was helping the pastor during the service and could not sit by me.

Another friend too said he was doing something else. I got very upset. I felt shattered that good friends who could see my need and who knew how much I was wanting to learn could do it to me. I wrote a letter saying how I felt and that the young people were reserved towards me. This was duly discussed by everyone and for a while a bit more effort was made.

Some weeks later there were three more cancellations. I was very upset again. I had really put my head down and studied the Bible and tried hard. I was not angry with anyone. I just felt let down and despairing. The blackness of my feelings swept over me. The time had come for me to show the young people by some visual aid, the depths of my feelings. I had thought of it some time before. I found some black cloth and wrapped it round my wrist for all to see. The black wrist was a cry from my heart. Please try to understand what it is like to be deaf. My thoughts poured out of my head.

> Why are the youth getting worse? Why, but how? For I know some of them hate me, but I love them all. Heart to heart you can love God but why do you leave me alone? I do not want you to leave me alone. There is nothing in my mind but I've got a pain. I will run a risk. It was not only the pain but like lost memories. How do I know? I ask you why are you not helping me with the Bible? I want to know more in the Bible. I will never give up Christ. But I do not want to do everything by myself. I am with Jesus, yesterday, today and forever, as well as you are. Praying always, 'Do not be a Black Wrist that makes me become a trouble-maker. Do not ask me about the Black Wrist in case I might fall into pain. I am about to fall. I love you all'.

Now my secret was out. Now everyone knew about the Black Wrist. Four times I have felt the dark despair of the Black Wrist. Once when I had the accident to my cheek bone, once in Margate, when I left college, and now.

> Who can help me? No one wants to do it all the time. How? I think perhaps they need money to do it. Then I would not have them. How can I understand the minister speaking to us? How can I understand it? Not many Christians helped me. Do not say, 'What about the others?' I will choose one if they are good at spelling and understanding words from the minister. During most meetings I read Christian books but do not say 'Good lad!' to me. I don't want to have to read during a service. I want help to understand what the minister says. That would be better than reading. I want to know about more new words from the Bible that I have not seen before. Who can help me?
>   I cannot move to another church until God tells me. I cannot go to a deaf church. This is difficult for me to understand. Because I have been with all of you for more

than five years. Am I lonely? Is it true? I am the only deaf person in this church. I am totally deaf. I am totally deaf.

If my cry for help fails I would like to marry, then she can hear for me and help me. She would not make a fuss about it. If she said that we would have deaf children I will explain to her that that is not so. As I was hearing at birth, I can have hearing children. If I had a deaf child I would ask the Lord to heal him.

The story of the Black Wrist is over. I give up my secret. Oh Lord I love them all. My book is nearly finished but I must tell you one more incident which happened to me one day when I was away at a youth camp held at the International Bible Training Institute. One Sunday I told my leader that I would not come to the last service. I had found the weekend tiring trying to lip read lectures for so long. I wanted time to be by myself. I went into the chapel on my own. First of all I cleaned up the room, put all the chairs back into their right places. There were some black, soft armchairs like those used in Mastermind. There was one big arm chair which can swivel round. I put it facing the wall. I sat in the small one. The big one was not facing me. I settled down to read a book. I read one page for about ten minutes. I was too upset with the way the weekend had gone. The pain of despair filled me. I put the book down and took up my Bible. I read and read turning over the pages and looking at various verses and chapters. Suddenly I looked up and saw that the big black chair was now facing me. I was amazed at it. It must be Jesus sitting on it and talking to me. First of all I could not believe it then I thought about it.

I looked at the chair a little longer. It made me think. 'One thing is sure, Jesus loves you.' I believe that Jesus was sitting there talking to me. I had not touched the chair. I was amazed at it. I praised the Lord because I had never seen anything like it before. I thought of the verse, 'And we know that in all things God works for the good of those who

love him, who have been called according to his purpose'
(Romans 8:28).

This experience reminded me again of the personal love
and care Jesus has for me and for all of us. It made me feel
loved and wanted again.

Looking back over what I have written about the black
wrist and my dark despair, I can see that some readers will
find my experiences hard to understand. Does Jesus make
any difference to my life? It is a mistake to think that the
moment you become a Christian every problem disappears
and that we somehow lose our natural feelings and frustrations. I have begun to learn that by walking with the Lord
and sharing my despair with him, my pain has gradually
been eased. Since the sad days of the black wrist, many
things have happened and I have discovered that the Lord's
unfailing love is everlasting. As I have obeyed him I have
felt more at peace. Slowly my life has become calmer. I
have learned that as I take each new experience step by
step with the Lord, so he leads me on to something
new.

I have gone away for several weekend courses with my
friends from the youth group to the International Bible
Training Institute. These weekends have been very great
experiences for me, and it's been encouraging that I have
been able to follow almost everything that was said. Most
of the sessions were on boy-girl relationships, subjects
which kept us all listening intently. It is good to have clear
teaching from the Bible and it makes me realise how
important it is to wait for God's perfect timing about
getting married. Surely it is only worth thinking of marriage
if the Lord leads clearly. I believe he will have someone
very special for me. I do not want to miss the best the Lord
has by rushing into a friendship too soon. Whoever marries
me will have to have a sense of humour and a lot of
patience! Perhaps she too will be deaf. I do not know. All I
do know is that this is an area in my life where I must listen
and obey the Lord very carefully.

I have also learned to drive which has opened up a whole

new world to me. I enjoyed all my lessons and even on my first outing with the instructor I did not make a kangaroo start. I changed gears smoothly from one to another. The whole process seemed to come easily to me. My driving teacher was very good, a nice small man, a very special person for deaf drivers. He was patient and had ideas on how to explain things to me. For example, he told me that the rev counter was a great help to deaf people. It was true. It helped me understand the engine speeds and so I was able to change gears without jerking. He was an excellent teacher.

Then came the day of the test. It was a beautifully sunny day in autumn and the sky was blue. Many friends were praying for me that I would concentrate and drive well. Everything went smoothly except for one mistake. When we came to the end of the test I held my breath. Had I passed or hadn't I? The tester smiled at me and handed me the result. I had passed.

I was so joyful. I will sing in the shadow of the Lord's wings. The Lord had helped me with my driving test. Thank you Lord for loving me.

Some people are surprised that it is safe for a deaf person to drive. In many ways it is safer than for a hearing person. Of course I have to look in all my mirrors more often. I have to be extra careful as I cannot hear traffic coming up behind me, or an ambulance or police siren. But I can concentrate. No one can speak to me while I am driving because I cannot turn to them to lip read, so I have no distractions. I can keep my eyes on the road. I have noticed when I am a passenger in other cars that very often the driver is so busy chatting, he does not watch the road the whole time. Sometimes I have even seen drivers turn round to speak to someone in the back seat.

Having passed my test, the next thing was to buy a car. I had been saving hard. At last I saw the type of car I wanted, a gold Ford Fiesta, second-hand but in very good condition. I enjoyed driving it home and swishing up the drive and parking it for the first time. What plans I had to take my

friends out. What adventures I would have, now that I was
free to drive off whenever I liked. I soon discovered how
expensive a car is to run. But by being careful I get plenty of
enjoyment from it. It feels good to be in charge as I drive
through the countryside. I've even driven up to London
and managed to come back from Piccadilly and Trafalgar
Square without a scratch.

Passengers in my car soon learn to talk amongst themselves. If I have only one friend in the car I slot in a cassette
for them to enjoy. I realise it must seem a silent journey to
them, as they cannot speak to me. It is useful having
passengers at times. They tell me if the engine sounds
wrong or if there are strange noises in other parts of the
car.

One of my proudest moments was when I drove my car
over to my old school. I parked it amongst the staff cars and
strolled in to see my former teachers. They came out to
inspect it and have their photos taken. It was good to go
back to see them and to laugh about school days. They
produced all sorts of interesting sports awards I'd won, and
pieces of work which I'd long forgotten. 'Do you remember
this . . .? Do you remember when . . .?' we kept saying to
each other. One of the teachers had brought with him a
page of writing from his ten-year-old son who still remembered the way I had taught him cricket five years before. He
had enjoyed it so much that when he heard I was returning
to visit his father, he sat down and wrote to me. Here is part
of his account of his day.

When Phillip said 'hello' his speech sounded different. I
was surprised because he was the first deaf person I'd
spoken to. He was tall and easy to get on with. Phillip
showed me around the school. He had a sense of
humour. Phillip had arranged to play cricket with me
after dinner. I rushed through my dinner to get to the
field. I beat my Dad eating lunch. I didn't know anything
about cricket and Phillip taught me. He was a very good
teacher and very patient. We got on quite well except I

was too small for the bat. Phillip whacked the ball into
the bushes, so we spent ages looking for it.

Christopher Sharpe

I was surprised that Christopher remembered so much of
that day. It felt rather strange sitting in my old classroom
drinking a cup of coffee where once I had been struggling
with maths and history. I realised then how much I owed to
Mr Sharpe and Mrs Edwards who had worked so hard with
me.

My book has shown many sad and difficult moments as
well as amusing incidents. Today I am happy with the Lord.
I know I have still a lot to learn about him, but so many
things have changed. He helps me a lot and I love him too.
As the title of my book says, I cannot hear you, but I can
hear God, with all my heart. But Jesus does not only love
me. It is the same for everyone. Whether you can hear or
whether you are deaf, Jesus is the same yesterday today
and for ever. He can help you too.

All of us in the past have been prodigal sons, because we
did not know Jesus. We did not see him. When I was just a
child, I left for the wilds, without knowing much about
Jesus. I became like a runaway son because I did not know
him. Nobody had told me about him and I gave him no
thought as I began to live my lazy life in the wilds. Oh, what
an alien life I lived. Nobody looking at me then could have
told how well everything was going to work out. When I
heard a preacher telling people about Jesus, I was amazed
at what he had done. I thought over and over again, 'Who is
Jesus? Who was Jesus? Who is Jesus?' I had been about to
starve but I became like a prodigal son, the wasteful son.
Now I rejoice in the Lord's name all day long. I am glad and
rejoice with the Lord. My heart is glad and my tongue
rejoices. So I sing in the shadow of the Lord's wings. Jesus
is with me and with you too. We are not alone with him. We
are with him for ever. In the Lord's unfailing love, we shall
let him be our guide . . . Oh, Jesus loves me. Jesus loves
you. Jesus will help you. Be honest. Let the Holy Spirit

help you. Be open to him with all your heart. The son of
man must be lifted up so that *everyone* who believes in him
may have eternal life. So believe God's son, Jesus Christ,
with your whole heart. Life eternal is a gift. 'For God so
loved the world that he gave his one and only son that
whoever believes in him shall not perish but have eternal
life' (John 3:16). His love is everlasting. His loving kindness is everlasting. His faithfulness and his unfailing love
continues. Hallelujah!

These words explain just some of my thoughts which I
want to share. It took a long time to write them all down,
but I kept working regularly. Finally when my book was
finished it filled a large black file. I got various friends to
read it and they made corrections and suggestions. Without
their help and encouragement I don't think it would ever
have got finished. I was not sure where to send it, but I
knew someone who worked in Bedford Square in London.
And I knew that Hodder and Stoughton, the publishers,
also had offices there. Boldly I wrote a letter to the editor
and bundled up my precious book just as it was, with all its
corrections and hurried handwriting. I did not know then
how important it is to type a book out neatly to present it
attractively to the publisher.

I asked my friend to deliver it by hand for me. I did not
trust the post with it. A new editor had just arrived in the
religious books department. He was determined to read
every manuscript which came in. So bravely he tackled my
untidy scrawl. Perhaps even now I have not fully taken in
how amazing it was that he wrote to me saying he was
prepared to publish it.

Before long it was my turn to be crossing Bedford Square
and to be climbing up the flights of dusty stairs to discuss the
book with the editor. I thought it would be just a matter of
typing it out just as it was with perhaps a few spelling
corrections. I soon found that I needed to work through the
text again, explaining some events in more detail and
unravelling some of the more complicated paragraphs. It
took almost another year to do that, working at it in a

disciplined way week by week, when I came home from work. Now the great moment has come when it is being sent off to the printer. It goes with the hope that it will glorify God and that through it some readers will come to love and trust Jesus.

If anyone would like to write to me please write to the address below:

Phillip Hassall
P.O. Box 17
Tunbridge Wells.
Kent

'Insight into Deafness'

Deafness, however great or small is a cage of loneliness.
A feeling of sadness, of being left out – unknown to others.
It's a language all of its own unique in its garbled sounds.
Hearing is like a distorted radio or a tape playing backwards in a cassette recorder.
It's a hurt feeling when everyone laughed at the joke except you.
Deafness is weeping, crying in frustration to understand a voice;
And straining to see the lips move – the interpreter to ears.
Deafness is exhaustion from intense listening. It's a battle from beginning to end.
A struggle that is not noticed – because there is nothing to see.

By courtesy of Miss Barbara Head, Sanderstead.

Points to Remember When Talking to Deaf People

1 First of all you must get their attention. A gentle touch on the arm will do.

2 Never stand with your back to a window or bright lights – this means your face will be in the shade and difficult to lip read.

3 Make sure there are sufficient lights on. Candle light can be difficult!

4 Never talk with a pen, pencil or cigarette in your mouth; it distorts words.

5 Always have paper and pen ready to jot down words.

6 Look at the deaf person when you are speaking, do not turn away.

7 Try to keep to one subject in conversation. Give some warning if you are going to switch. It is difficult for a person lip reading to jump from football to summer holidays.

8 If you can see that you have not been understood, say the same things again, only rephrased, e.g. 'Haven't you finished your work yet?' rephrased to 'Have you finished your work?' (this is easier to lip read).

9 Speak in sentences not odd words. There should always be a contextual framework.

10 If you are going to spend a long time with a deaf person wear simple clothes: bright jazzy clothes distract the deaf person and make it hard to concentrate.

11 Only use sign language if you know the deaf person uses it. Some people can get very upset by its use. However, do not leave out your own normal gestures and expressions when you talk.